In *Kissing the Face of God,* a pastor's heart has served us with a desire to know God better. The human heart is His avenue of speaking to and drawing us to Himself, and Sam Hinn is here helping us with insights sensitizing us to such a possibility.

—JACK W. HAYFORD, FOUNDING PASTOR,
THE CHURCH ON THE WAY
CHANCELLOR, THE KING'S COLLEGE AND SEMINARY

Sam Hinn understands that worshiping God is the single most important thing we do. Worship is not just the doorway—it's the entire house.

—TED HAGGARD, SENIOR PASTOR, NEW LIFE CHURCH
COLORADO SPRINGS, COLORADO

You can't be around Sam Hinn without getting an insatiable appetite and hunger to pursue the face of God. His very life breathes worship, which is the way it is supposed to be. Our entire life is a call to worship God in everything we think, say, do and feel.

Who needs to read this book? Anyone who believes the admonition of St. Paul, who said, "We all with unveiled face beholding as in a mirror the glory of the Lord are being changed into that *same image* from glory to glory!" (See 2 Corinthians 3:18.)

—DR. MARK J. CHIRONNA
AUTHOR, *STEPPING INTO GREATNESS*
AND *BEYOND THE SHADOW OF DOUBT*

In *Kissing the Face of God,* Pastor Sam Hinn has allowed us to follow him from the feet of Jesus, worshiping Him as his Savior and Lord, into the very throne room of God. There, because of such a longing and beseeching cry for His presence, he was drawn into a face-to-face relationship with his Father. But as he kissed the face of God, he realized his Father had kissed him back. The desire of his heart for so long had been realized. God had kissed back!

—DR. FUCHSIA PICKETT, INTERNATIONAL SPEAKER/TEACHER
AUTHOR, *WORSHIP HIM* AND *PLACED IN HIS GLORY*

Few people have the ability to exercise leadership with the transparency and honesty that characterizes Sam Hinn. He is not afraid to show his struggles and efforts in his walk with God. Sam has the ability to be a spiritual coach who challenges and affirms others to believe that the best from God is attainable.

Allow yourself to be challenged by the truths revealing the religiosity that hurts all of us. Let passion ignite your heart once again. Heed the calling back to the mountaintop of God. Embrace these principles, which will become threads of love to bring you closer, much closer to the face of God—so you can kiss Him once again.

—DANILO MONTERO
INTERNATIONAL PSALMIST AND SPEAKER
BEST-SELLING AUTHOR

We live in a time when the glory of God has been touted to be present in too many meetings and too many conferences when it is not present at all. The sad result is that we are left with a saccharin-like taste in our mouth. We yawn when massive promises are pronounced, we cringe when we hear how God once moved, because we still taste the saccharin of the last moment God was said to have visited. However, there is a bright spot on the horizon. In *Kissing the Face of God* Sam Hinn has captured the essence of the before, during and after of God's glory. Reading this book will bring back the hope for a real visitation and what we must do to prepare for it.

—JOHN PAUL JACKSON
FOUNDER AND CHAIRMAN
STREAMS MINISTRIES INTERNATIONAL

# Kissing the Face of God

## SAM HINN

**Charisma**
HOUSE

KISSING THE FACE OF GOD by Sam Hinn
Published by Charisma House
A part of Strang Communications Company
600 Rinehart Road
Lake Mary, Florida 32746
www.charismahouse.com

Cover design by Karen Gonsalves

Library of Congress Cataloging-in-Publication Data

Hinn, Sam.
    Kissing the face of God / Sam Hinn.
        p. cm.
ISBN 0-88419-536-8 (trade paper)
1. God—Worship and love. 2. Desire for God. I. Title.
BV4817 .H56 2002
231.7—dc21

                                        2002011876


02 03 04 05 — 87654321
Printed in the United States of America

In loving memory of the man
I was honored to call my father,
Costandi Hinn
1924–1982

# Dedication

I affectionately dedicate this book to two wonderful women whose love and prayers have encouraged and helped to mold my life for me to kiss God's face. To my mom, Clemance, better known to us as "Yama," whose love and dedication to the Lord and her children have been a beacon of light to all of us. Her love for Jesus has not only inspired me to kiss the face of God, but also to kiss the face of my children with His love. Watching her love Jesus has taught me to fall in love with Him.

To my beautiful wife, Erika, my life and joy. You are and always will be God's greatest gift in my life. You are not only my honey, but also my greatest friend. Thank you for everything you do for the children and me. You are my world!

To my wonderful Savior, Jesus Christ. It will always be about You! My life, worship and family will always be because of You. Jesus, I love You!

# Acknowledgments

To my children, Samia, Costi, Michael and Christa—you are my encouragement. I live my life to be the best dad and friend I can be to you. I am forever indebted to you for helping shape my life. Thank you for loving and teaching me to be a good dad and friend. I love you more than this whole world.

A dear friend once said to me, "In this life you can never have too many friends." Over the years God has blessed my life with many wonderful friends whose lives have deeply touched mine. I could easily write another book just about them.

To my five brothers, Benny, William, Chris, Henry and Mike, and my two sisters, Rose and Mary—thank you for what you've instilled in my life about family.

To Larry Keefauver, my bro! Larry, words can never express my love and gratitude for the blessing you are in my life. Thank you for all your help and encouragement with this book. Bro, your life and ministry have been a living epistle.

To Dennis Davis—God has given me such a special friend in you. Dennis, you have deeply impacted my life. Your timely words from the Lord and your messages have left a mark on my life. Thank you, Dennis!

To Pastor Sherwood Wilson, Terry Mahan, Mark Chironna, Robert Stearns and Danilo Montero—thank you for showing me what covenant friendship really means.

To John and Edee Tamsett—before Jesus only heaven will reveal how you have touched my life. There are no words to convey my deepest love for how you have touched my life and blessed my family. Thank you showing me that Jesus loves me. Erika and I love you so much; thanks for the threes—love, prayer and friendship.

To the best and craziest bunch of elders who have made these past seven years of serving Jesus so much fun—thank you, Don Newman, Mark Meyers, James Ting, Jeff Welker, Chuck Blystone, Simon Tavanyar, Tom Gill and Ron Holmes. It's an honor serving the Lord with you!

To The Gathering Place staff, leaders and my church family—thank you for being such great sheep to shepherd. Thank you for loving, praying and supporting me. The past seven years have been the best years of my life in ministry because of you. I have told you this before—the Lord has given me the best church family on the planet. Now I want the world to know that I pastor the best sheep in the world. It is such an honor to minister the Word of God to you every week and to be called your pastor and friend.

To Jack Hayford, Ted Haggard, Fuchsia Pickett, Danilo Montero and John Paul Jackson—thanks for expressing your confidence in this message and helping others to kiss the face of God.

To the many friends and pastors who have not been mentioned by name but have no less touched my life and given me the honor of ministering in their pulpits—thank you for allowing God to use you to help shape my life and ministry. I wish I had room and could mention every one of you by name, but you know who you are. Thank you for touching my life; this book is because of you. I pray the best is yet to come for you. Thank you for serving Jesus!

To Stephen and Joy Strang—it is an honor to work with such a wonderful publisher. Steve and Joy, thank you for the years of encouragement, direction and, most of all, patience in working with me. Thank you, Barbara Dycus; you are a pleasure to work with.

# Contents

# Chapter 1

# *The* Longing Heart

"These are days of longing. I am going to bring you into a place of longing for Me," says the Lord. "I will become that all-surpassing gift in your life. I will bring you into the exceeding, abundant life of My Spirit. These are days of longing, either a longing for Me or a longing for things that do not pertain to Me. I am longing for you. Are you longing for Me as I am longing for you?" says the Lord. "These are days of longing. I am raising up a people of longing in these days. A people ruined for ordinary living, people of longing. I am looking for a people of longing." (I received this word from the Lord while ministering in Costa Rica, July 5, 2000.)

## Days of Unprecedented Hunger

I remember that night as if it were just yesterday. I had stayed up the entire night praying and asking God to give me a heart that would long for Him in the way God desired for me to long for Him. At

1

about 4:00 A.M. I began to study the Word, looking for scriptures that would speak and confirm this word that I received from the Lord.

What a time I had with the Lord that night! Before I knew it, it was time to go and minister in the morning session with my friend Danilo Montero. That morning I had the wonderful privilege to minister to about four hundred worship leaders, musicians and singers. The presence of God filled us. All of those wonderful worship leaders flooded the altar with tears in holy desperation for God's presence. Just as God filled them with a longing for His presence, I pray that this book will help and encourage you in your longing to know Him.

God wants to stir the hearts of His people in these days like never before. I believe with all my heart that the word I received that July day in Costa Rica is coming to pass in the hearts of many of God's people who are desperately hungry for more of God. We are living in a time when many people just can't explain what they are feeling or sensing in their spirit, but they are simply crying out, "God, there must be more!"

These are truly days of unprecedented hunger. While traveling and ministering these past few years, I have seen a longing on the faces of God's people. I am hearing a sound in worship that I have not ever heard before. I hear the sound of inspiring songs being sung, but I hear more than the music—I am hearing a sound of longing. Preachers are teaching about this hunger; leaders are trying to explain it. But for me, no message can truly explain or satisfy this longing. It's a longing only God can satisfy. As I think about the hunger I have witnessed—and experience that longing in the depths of my own being—I am reminded of the words of Jesus:

> Blessed are those who hunger and thirst for righteousness, for they shall be filled.
>
> —MATTHEW 5:6

## Longing As God Longs

My heart is so stirred because we are living in a day when God is deepening *our* longings for Him by allowing us to experience the deep longing He has to have an intimate relationship with His own. As we begin to experience the intensity of God's longing within us, the church will begin to look and sound different. This has happened to me. I have never experienced such holy desperation for more of God in my life and family as I am experiencing now.

> God wants to stir the hearts of His people in these days like never before.

The past few years have been life-changing years for me. God's people today seem to be in a place of tremendous longing for more of God's life and presence in their life. Since writing my book *Changed in His Presence* a number of years ago, I have experienced an incredible journey in His presence.[1]

I believe that you, with me, are hungrier for God today than you have ever been. Recently, the cry of my heart has been, "God, there must be more! There must be more to You than what I have experienced, than what I have seen in the church, than what I have experienced in ministry."

At this moment I am praying:

> *Father, I am so hungry for You. Even while writing this opening chapter, I know that there must be more. There must be more to You; there must be more of You. I ask You to touch my life even while I write. Lord, please touch every life that reads this book with the life of the Holy Spirit, and give us a greater longing for You than we have ever had or known.*

As I write, I am praying for you. It is my deepest prayer that God will touch your heart with His living presence and that, while you read, the deep work of the Holy Spirit will deepen the longing of your heart for Him. I know this: The deep things of God are calling for the deep things in us. Allow the Holy Spirit to create in you this deep longing for God in a greater way than you have ever experienced.

For the last six years, at the beginning of each new year I have asked the Lord to give me a scripture from His Word that would be my yearlong desire in prayer and study. As 2001 drew to a close and we prepared to enter into 2002, the Holy Spirit spoke to my heart with the words of Psalm 27:4–8:

> One thing I have desired of the LORD,
> That will I seek:
> That I may dwell in the house of the LORD
> All the days of my life,
> To behold the beauty of the LORD,
> And to inquire in His temple.
> For in the time of trouble
> He shall hide me in His pavilion;

In the secret place of His tabernacle
He shall hide me;
He shall set me high upon a rock.

And now my head shall be lifted up above my
    enemies all around me;
Therefore I will offer sacrifices of joy in His
    tabernacle;
I will sing, yes, I will sing praises to the LORD.

Hear, O LORD, when I cry with my voice!
Have mercy also upon me, and answer me.
When You said, "Seek My face,"
My heart said to You, "Your face, LORD, I will
    seek."

Since the beginning of 2002, I have been praying and mediating on these words. God continually pours out life and revelation each time I reread these verses. He encourages me that He will satisfy this longing in me.

## One Thing I Have Desired

David speaks of "*one thing* I have desired of the LORD, that will I seek." Take a moment to stop and reflect on those words! Ask yourself:

- What is my greatest desire?
- What is my heart longing for most right now?
- What is that *one thing* that is driving my passion?

Is your passion driving you into a deeper relationship with God, or is it driving you away from Him?

Recently as I ministered in another church, the

presence of God became very real as we were worshiping. His presence seemed to get heavier and heavier upon me. During those moments, the Lord breathed words to me that were life-changing. "I will make you a minister of Jesus," He whispered into my spirit. My heart was so overwhelmed.

"Lord," I responded, "what an honor You have given me to call me to be Your minister."

Then He said, "Sam, for the purpose and cause of eternity, in every relationship, your purpose must be focused on the eternal—not just for the now. Sam, all that you do is for the sake of eternity."

## Allow the Holy Spirit to create a deep longing for God greater than you have ever experienced.

In that moment everything became crystal clear. I now knew God's purpose for my life…for every relationship…for every place I go…for every time of ministry…for every person I meet. I must know the *one thing*. It all must be for the purpose and cause of eternity!

Ever since that day that *one thing* has become my driving passion. It has eliminated distractions and wants, and it has given me a single focus for my whole being. I am on the right track! I am in pursuit with every affection, "for the purpose and cause of eternity." If what I am doing is *not* for eternity's cause and purpose, I must stop. If what I'm about to say isn't for eternity, I will not say it. My every act and word must now count for God's eternal cause and purpose.

## Life's Greatest Desire

David's life desire could not be equated with his kingdom, his wealth or his position as king. His desire surpassed all others in his heart. His three-fold desire consumed his being. David's desire included:

1. *A desire for the presence of God.* "One thing I have desired of the Lord." It was not a desire that could be fulfilled by ministry opportunities, denominational acceptance or even by church affiliation. Nothing in all of life could compare with David's desire for God's presence, a desire birthed in him from the Lord.

2. *A desire to dwell in God's house.* David came to the understanding that God's presence would arise from dwelling in God's house. From there he would behold the beauty of the Lord.

3. *A desire to inquire in His temple.* Dwelling in God's house and desiring His presence would become David's place of protection. "For in the time of trouble He shall hide me in His pavilion; in the secret place of His tabernacle He shall hide me; He shall set me high upon a rock" (Ps. 27:5).

Above all else in life, David had fixed his heart's desire on this one thing. Getting power, wealth, prominence and fame could not satisfy his heart's desire, the greatest need of his life. Only God's presence could! I wonder if in all of our getting, are we getting what we really need?

David desired and waited. He sought after God's presence and prayed. He spent time in God's house for all of the right reasons. David wasn't in God's house because of any other reason than being intimate with God.

## David dwelled in God's house to behold the beauty of the Lord—not to receive the blessing of man.

Why do we go to God's house? Are we there because of the preacher or because the music is better than in some other place? Do we go to God's house to be seen or because there is a special service in which a noted minister will anoint people with oil for healing or will prophesy over us? Are we in God's house because of great programs, wonderful traditions, powerful leaders or effective ministry for our children or youth?

None of these reasons would have motivated David. David dwelled in God's house to behold the beauty of the Lord—not to receive the blessing of man. He loved God and just wanted to behold His beauty and to inquire in His temple.

## Having a Heart for God

If we really desire intimacy and communion with God, we will position our hearts with all diligence to seek after Him. A study of Scripture reveals that King David didn't have a burning bush experience like

Moses. He didn't see the Lord high and lifted up like Isaiah. He didn't have a vision as John had on the isle of Patmos. He wasn't knocked off his horse like Saul of Tarsus with the blinding glory of God.

Like David, many of us may never see or have a burning bush encounter like Moses. We may never see the blinding glory of God in the face of Jesus Christ like Saul. But even though we have not had these kinds of manifestations in our lives, we can behold the beauty of the Lord every day by deepening our worship and longing for Him.

## A Heart After God

What is required of those who long after God? God gives us a great example with David, whose life was filled with failures and mistakes. Something very special about David touched the heart of God. What was it? It was David's heart for God!

When David penned Psalm 27, he was a wealthy king. During this time his kingdom and lands were prosperous. Yet in the midst of all his responsibilities as king, the wealthy ruler had one supreme desire: "The one thing I ask of the LORD—the thing I seek most—is to live in the house of the LORD all the days of my life, delighting in the LORD's perfections and meditating in his Temple" (Ps. 27:4, NLT).

I wonder if in the midst of all of his royalty, wealth and position, if just for a moment David reflected back to those earlier years when the Lord touched him as a simple, young shepherd boy in the field.

David was a *man after God's heart*. Samuel

declared this to the hardened and rebellious King Saul: "But now your kingdom shall not continue. The LORD has sought for Himself a man after His own heart, and the LORD has commanded him to be commander over His people, because you have not kept what the LORD commanded you" (1 Sam. 13:14). A real heart for God longs after God's heart. David had a passionate, insatiable longing in his heart for the heart of God.

God had given His heart to David because David had already given his entire heart to God. He desired the heart of God so much that he was willing to discard his own. No matter how busy his life had become, or how much of this world's wealth and material possessions he had accumulated, his greatest desire was to possess the heart of God. He would give it all to gain God. How much of your heart are you willing to give away to God?

Today many people are so stressed out that they are merely living to make a living. They are unable to rise above the problems and worries that weigh them down. Because they are unable to escape the mundane, their lives have become dull and boring.

My heart breaks for people like this, people who just want to escape their mundane existences, if only for a moment. My friend, if this is you, please hear me. God wants to place a burning desire in you for Him. He will remove every stumbling block that stands in the way of your heart. But it begins with giving your heart away and receiving, in its place, the heart of God. Will you give your heart away? Are you willing to surrender your heart for His?

Only in Him can your burdens be laid aside and your heart come into true rest. Why continue to struggle and live in inner turmoil? Right now, give your heart to God, and He will give you a new heart, a heart that belongs to Him. No better time than right now exists to surrender your heart to Him in a new and living way. As you give your heart away to Him, He in turn gives His heart to you!

> A real heart for God
> longs after God's heart.

What did God see when He looked at the heart of David?

- David had an undivided heart, a heart that sought God (Ps. 86:11).

- David had a contrite heart, a heart that was broken before God (Ps. 51:17).

- David had a clean heart before God (Ps. 51:9–10).

David's heart cried out for God. You can cry out for the living God with the same intensity and passion as David did. You can be a man or a woman after the heart of God. Make David's cry your own:

> How lovely is Your tabernacle, O LORD of hosts!
> My soul longs, yes, even faints,
> For the courts of the LORD;
> My heart and my flesh cry out for the living God.
>
> —PSALM 84:1–2

# For What Are You Longing?

We live in a time and place where people have all
sorts of longings in their souls. There doesn't seem to
be a difference between those who are of the household of faith and those who are not. People are longing for all sorts of things. Some long for these things
just to escape from the pressures of life. Some just
exist, never tasting the real depths of life. Some live
longing for riches and wealth, while others are longing just to make a living. Others are living to climb
the ladder of success and don't care how many
people they step on while trying to reach their goal.

Many in the body of Christ are living for all the
wrong reasons. Today many in the church are longing more for ministry than for an intimate relationship with God. People are longing for the gifts of the
Holy Spirit, yet they don't know Him as a person.
They want His gifts, His power and His miracles, but
they are blind to His person. Some will run and
chase after ministry gifts in the body of Christ, driving hundreds of miles to receive a word or a prayer
from a guest minister. But these same individuals
will not travel eighteen inches to get on their knees
in prayer to meet the Holy Spirit as a person.

God is seeking a church that is seeking and longing
after Him. Many attend church looking for anointing
and gifts or for messages to motivate and pump them
up, only to leave the same way they came because
they did not come seeking the One who seeks them.
Seeking revival and the outpouring of the Holy Spirit
is well and good, but we cannot forget that God is
seeking for men and women after His own heart.

## The Heart God Seeks After

Out of David's heart—*a heart after God*—came this cry: "As the deer pants for the water brooks, so pants my soul for You, O God. My soul thirsts for God, for the living God. When shall I come and appear before God?" (Ps. 42:1–2).

> God is seeking a church that is seeking and longing after Him.

A deer often feeds near the water brook where the vegetation is plenteous and the water is satisfying. But when the deer is being hunted, with its predator in full pursuit, it becomes parched with thirst. Almost spent, it plunges into the water brook as its last refuge. Understand this lesson from life. When a deer is exhausted from being the hunted, his last refuge is to plunge into the water. So it is with us when we are exhausted from the dealings of this world. We find our hiding place, our resting place, in God.

In this psalm we observe that David is heartsick. His most urgent need was communion with God. How about you? Are you heartsick and desperately needing communion with God?

What was it about David's heart that got God's attention? When David was in the Judean desert he prayed, "O God, you are my God, earnestly I seek you; my soul thirsts for you, my body longs for you, in a dry and weary land where there is no water. I have seen you in the sanctuary and beheld your power and your glory" (Ps. 63:1–2, NIV).

When David penned this psalm he was in a dry and barren wilderness, far from the sanctuary, his family and his friends. Yet even in the wilderness he longed for God. David's deepest desire was for communion with his God. The whole of his being was longing for communion with God. His life was as dry as arid land bereft of water.

Like the deer that sought the refuge of the water brook in Psalm 42, David was seeking communion with God as his refuge. We must do the same. Whether we are being pursued by the enemy, or our lives are being threatened by external circumstances and threat, or we are dry and parched within from a desert experience, our desire for refuge should be the communion of God.

## Never Curse Your Wilderness

Every great servant of God has found himself in the desert, including Jesus. You will experience the wilderness as God's gift. In the wilderness you will learn to thirst and hunger after Him. The lesson of the wilderness teaches you just how much you need Him.

A few years ago my wife and I were driving from Orlando, Florida, to Cleveland, Tennessee, to be with some dear friends. We had just crossed the Florida border into Georgia, a beautiful drive with very pleasant sights along the road. Suddenly we hit a long stretch of highway that was totally barren. I felt as if we were playing a game my kids used to play called "Where in the World Is Carmen Sandiego?" But our game was called "Where in the World Are Sam and Erika?"

I wondered where the trees, nice landscaping and buildings had gone. It was as if we had crossed the line into the land of nothingness. All I could think about as we drove this long stretch of barren road was how thankful I was that Erika and I have a lot in common to talk about, so it wasn't going to be a long, lonely drive.

That stretch of road reminded me of the many times in my life when it seems as if everything is going along just fine. My life seems well land-scaped, and things seem to be just great. But sud-denly the scene changes. At those moments I feel like asking, "Where did the nice trees and land-scapes go?" In my heart I know that I have just left the plush meadows of my walk with God to step into the dry barrenness of the wilderness.

When things are going great, it's easy to think you really don't need God. But God has creative ways to remind you of just how much you need Him. Stepping into the wilderness is one of those ways. It's amazing to me how much we cry out and need God in the wilderness.

At times it will take a wilderness to bring you to the place of total desperation for God. You are not alone! Every great, godly leader has discovered this truth: Being distanced from life's comforts means being in a place where only God can help.

The only cry that brings comfort in the wilderness is, "O God, You are my God." David stirred himself up and took hold of God in his wilderness. You must recognize God in every circumstance you face. He must be the God of every moment of your life.

Even in the middle of your wilderness, He is
*Emmanuel*, "God with us." He will be your comfort
as He brings you through your desert experience.

In Psalm 63, David reveals a great life lesson. In
the midst of barren and dry land, David thirsted for
more than water. David cried out, "My soul thirsts
for You; my flesh longs for You in a dry and thirsty
land where there is no water" (Ps. 63:1). When
nearly everyone else would be longing for water to
sustain him, or perhaps for strength to make it,
David longed for God.

## At times it will take a wilderness to bring you to the place of total desperation for God.

Can you recall a time when your longing for God
caused you to thirst for Him with your whole being?
I can only imagine the intense pain David felt when
he cried out, "My heart and my flesh cry out for the
living God" (Ps. 84:2). Sadly, I don't remember very
many times in my own life when this was true of
me. How about you? Do you remember a time
when your longing for God became so intense that
you experienced physical pain?

Today so many people come to our church sanctu-
aries longing to meet the living God. Instead they are
merely introduced to the preacher or told about all
the programs available to them. I don't know about
you, but I want to see a lot more seeking for God taking place in the church. There is no program…no
sermon…and no music that can substitute for the
presence of God in our worship experience.

So I have looked for You in the sanctuary,
To see Your power and Your glory.

—PSALM 63:2

People today are hungry to know God. People are longing to see the power and glory of God. The glory of God is the result of the manifestation of the presence of God. Power and glory are to come together. God wants to manifest His power and glory in your life more than you desire it yourself.

I want you to know that God loves you so much. When you are going through the most painful times in your life and don't have the strength to pray the way you know you can, God even promises to give His attention to your sighs. When all you can do in prayer is sigh, "O God," the Lord hears your cry. "Lord, all my desire is before You; and my sighing is not hidden from You" (Ps. 38:9).

## Is There Life in Your Sanctuary?

What do you think about God's house? Is there life in the sanctuary? No matter whether the experiences we have had in church are good or bad, God loves His house! David recognized something that we need to take hold of in our hearts. He recognized that worship is not merely going to church and sitting in a nice song service. Worship is not just about music or the Word being preached—as important as God's Word is.

What was David's desire? What was he thirsting after?

As the deer pants for the water brooks,

So pants my soul for You, O God.
My soul thirsts for God, for the living God.
When shall I come and appear before God?

—PSALM 42:1–2

David's cry was not for water or for shade. David panted after God; he thirsted for God—not for the *things of God*, but for *God alone*.

David's longing for God was far more than an expression; he actively sought God. Our cry today might sound something like this: "Hey, when can I meet up with You, God? Hey, God, I need an appointment with You."

## David thirsted for God—not for the *things of God*, but for *God alone*.

What would worship in the house of God be like if we saw it as our appointment with God? Some people would never miss a doctor's appointment, but they feel no remorse at all about missing the house of God. What would our lives be like…what would the church look like…if we saw worship as an audience with the living God? If we treated worship as an appearance before God Himself, our worship would look and sound totally different. Worship after the heart of God delights in God.

As I have written this chapter, a strange occurrence has taken place. I have actually cried for you! I believe the Holy Spirit wants me to pray for you. As I close this chapter with a prayer, make the following scripture the cry of your own heart:

Whom have I in heaven but You?
And there is none upon earth that I desire
  besides You.
My flesh and my heart fail;
But God is the strength of my heart and my
  portion forever.
                                              —PSALM 73:25–26

There is no need to wait another minute. Please
agree with me as I pray for you.

*Father, in the name of Jesus, I lift up my brothers
and sisters who read this book. Touch them with
the Holy Spirit. Lord Jesus, take them deeper in
You. Remove every hindrance from their way. By
the power of your Holy Spirit I ask that you heal
them and cause them to hunger after You, O God!*

*Holy Spirit, we long to know God. Our hearts
are crying out, "O, that we may know Him."
Today we lift our hands to You. Our hearts long for
You as the dry land thirsts for water. Lord Jesus,
take our longings for God and put Your own longings deep within us. In Jesus' name I pray. Amen!*

## Chapter 2

# *What* Hinders *True* Worship?

C an you remember a time or place in your life that represents a landmark decision...a defining moment with God? Most of us look back to what the Lord has done in and through us with tremendous gratitude. In my own life, God has blessed many of my years with unspeakable experiences, dreams and words from heaven.

As I look back over my experiences, one year comes to mind as just such a landmark year. During that year God did a very deep work in my heart and life. Every message, teaching and worship experience was greatly anointed by God. Even this book, I believe, was birthed in 1986.

Early one Monday morning at the beginning of December in 1986, as I was preparing to lead our morning prayer meeting, the Lord said to me, "I want you to worship Me this morning."

I could have never imagined how that one word from the Lord would change my life forever. My life changed because of an encounter I had with Jesus.

In fact, it was more than an encounter—it was a vision of the Lord. That vision has forever changed my heart, my life and ministry. That defining moment and vision birthed my life's purpose.

In January of 1987, my brother Willie, a friend and I attended a James Robison Bible Conference in Dallas. I was so hungry for God after having the vision of the Lord in December 1986 that I would go anywhere to learn more about Him. I had never had this kind of hunger before, and I gladly jumped at the opportunity to attend this conference with Willie. I attended every meeting that I could. I couldn't get enough of the worship and the Word from speakers like Rick Godwin, Oral Roberts, Jack Hayford, James Robison and others. I remember soaking up every message that these wonderful servants of God preached.

On Thursday night, the presence of God was unlike anything I had ever experienced. I found myself in a heightened state of awareness of Him. The worship was incredible, and the ministry was great. But I couldn't wait for the altar time. I had decided that no matter what the altar call was about, I was going forward.

At the end of the service James Robison invited ministers, leaders and people to come and get their hearts right with God. My moment had come. I couldn't even wait for him to finish the invitation. I ran to the altar and was the third person to arrive. I was so hungry for God that I had wanted to be the first person there. I knelt down as James continued to encourage people to come and allow the Lord to minister to them.

As I knelt, the presence of God intensified and became very real and tangible. I began to cry (which is not difficult for me anyway) as I felt the presence of God becoming stronger and stronger. Something different was happening inside of me than what had happened just a month before. Time seemed to stand still. Eternity saturated both the atmosphere around me and my being deep within. The worship in that auditorium was electrifying to me. The presence of God in that corporate setting was unlike anything I had ever encountered.[1]

## Three Desperate Questions

I knew the presence of Jesus was in that meeting. As I knelt there before the Lord, three questions arose from my spirit, questions for which I desperately needed answers. I asked the Lord these three questions, and the answers He gave further defined the life-changing impact of the vision God had given me the previous month.

### Question #1—"Lord Jesus, why is the worship in this place so pure?"

To my first question, the Lord answered, "Sam, I will answer your first question. I want you to look all around you; look around this arena." I remember His words to me as if it were yesterday when I first heard them. I popped my head up and looked all around the place. Some people were standing while others were still sitting—but everyone was worshiping Jesus.

God said, "Do you want to know why the worship is so pure here? There are seven thousand people here from forty-eight different states. The reason worship is so pure is because they don't know each other. They haven't had time to get angry or bitter with one another. This is why the worship is so pure."

These words pierced my heart, and I knew immediately what the Lord was saying to me. I have been in many churches where there seemed to be such a resistance in the worship while the people are worshiping God. The people sing, but the worship goes nowhere. It simply becomes a time filler for something else. During worship people are looking around, seeing who is sitting on the front row or deciding it's time to go to the bathroom.

Over the years as I have learned a little more about worship, the presence of God and the Holy Spirit, I have come to learn that in every service the Holy Spirit has set a level for us to ascend in worship. Once we have reached this place of pure worship from the heart, the Holy Spirit begins to touch and change the hearts of the people.

When we come to worship God with bitterness, anger or offense filling our hearts, not only is our worship affected, but also we often leave the way we came—unable to receive from God because of the condition of our hearts.

### Question #2—"What comes after worship?"

Then God answered my second question. "The answer to your second question is *the dance*. This is what comes after worship." In that moment I looked up at the platform, and the lady leading worship began to dance. Then Betty Robison joined her, and both of them seemed to be like two little girls just dancing and twirling. They didn't have a care in this world. I sat there watching this incredible scene, aware that the Lord had just described the scene I was now witnessing.

Even more incredible was the fact that the presence of the Lord that I had felt during the early part of the service was now getting thicker and thicker. As the ladies were dancing and twirling in circles before the Lord, a wave of God's presence would hit everyone in the place each time Betty Robison waved her hand as she was dancing.

The presence of God flowed from the platform like a wave moving out into the whole arena. And with each wave His presence thickened.

The atmosphere in the entire arena was filled with joy. This dance was not a hyped-up thing, an in-the-flesh kind of dance with music as the focus. This was a dance in which the heart danced as we moved into deeper worship. It was as if a well of joy had been unstopped in the hearts of God's people. There is no other way to describe it. It was better than any party I had ever been to. Pure joy filled my heart that night.

### Question #3—"What are You going to do with my life?"

The answer to the third question was very personal. I'm not ready to share it yet because there are still things I am waiting on God to do in my life. (Thank you for understanding.)

God had so graciously recognized the desperation in my spirit to experience Him in a greater way than ever before. He had responded to the very specific need I had to receive these answers from Him. He will do the same for you. He will impact your life with a vision of Him that will be life changing! And He will increase your understanding of Him in very personal ways.

## The New Realm of God's Glory

I believe we are entering into a realm of God's presence and glory unlike anything we have ever seen. This coming realm of God's glory will fill the church, and people's lives will be shaken by the power of God. Waves of His glory will sweep through us, and we will never be the same again.

The arrival of God's glory among us always demands change. When His glory sweeps over His people, we cannot be weighed down with sin, anger or bitterness. All of these weights will become like spiritual gravity to keep us from ascending into the glory of God. His glory will expose any areas in our lives that have hindered us from worshiping God.

## The War Over Worship

As you worship God, war is raging against you. The enemy hates your worship. He wants to stop you from praising and worshiping God. The battle is not only personal; it's corporate. The whole church is at war.

Why is this war brewing against you and the body of Christ? In the battle, the enemy is attempting to distract you from the God's calling and vision for you. But do not take your eyes off Jesus. He is going to deliver you. Satan's simple tactic is to attack you so intensely that you will take your eyes Jesus—even if only for a moment.

Remember that not only were you *called* to ministry; you were also *created* to worship God. You may have been fighting this war without really knowing why. You may feel as though you have been continually distracted from worshiping the Lord as you would like to worship Him. Perhaps you even find it difficult to concentrate on worship when you come before the Lord—either corporately with the body of Christ or in your personal worship times at home. If you are fighting this battle right now, I want you to know that God is going deliver you. He will put His song back in your heart. God's best is yet to come, but we have to do some housecleaning first!

David, perhaps the greatest worshiper in Old Testament times, felt the impact of this battle as he tried to worship the Lord. His cries to the Lord can become our own cries as we fight through to experience God's presence:

> I cried out to You, O LORD:
> I said, "You are my refuge,
> My portion in the land of the living.
> Attend to my cry,
> For I am brought very low;
> Deliver me from my persecutors,
> For they are stronger than I.
> Bring my soul out of prison,
> That I may praise Your name;
> The righteous shall surround me,
> For You shall deal bountifully with me."
> —PSALM 142:5–7

Have mercy on me, O LORD!
Consider my trouble from those who hate me,
You who lift me up from the gates of death,
That I may tell of all Your praise
In the gates of the daughter of Zion.
I will rejoice in Your salvation.
—PSALM 9:13–14

Hindrances will arise to prevent your worship. Earlier in this chapter I shared with you about what happened to me at the James Robison Bible Conference. The Lord showed me that the worship was so pure in that setting because the seven thousand people gathered together had no time to get angry with one another or to become bitter with each other. Because the enemy had not been able to distract them from worship, they entered God's presence with pure hearts and unshackled spirits.

> Remember that not only were you *called* to ministry; you were also *created* to worship.

The enemy will war with you in every area of your life. He does not want you to worship God. He will war in your body with sickness. He will attack your soul with heaviness and pain. Satan will attack your mind with evil thoughts, not only when you are awake, but also as you sleep. He will do anything to keep you from worshiping God!

Why does the enemy battle so hard to keep you and me from worshiping God? Because worship is not something you are called to do. Worship is at the core of who you were created to be. God

designed you to be a worshiper. God doesn't want
you merely to set aside *times of worship* as a part of
your life. He desires for *your entire life to become worship to Him.*

Worship is not a church service or the singing of
hymns. Worship isn't led by singers or with instruments. Worship can never become just a part of the
week, or an hour on Sunday, when you pause from
life to give a token of time and money to God.
Worship is the all-consuming, never-ending focus
of your life. Worship is your calling as a child of
God. Worship is your life's orientation, which turns
your face from worldly pursuits and concerns to
God. Worship is a life totally consumed with a passionate love for God. Worship is a life that is continually kissing the face of God.

# Worship Is the Believer's Highest Calling

There are some big giants to battle against in the
land of worship. God will reveal the names of the
giants and give you the plan for your victory. But
first we must decide that worship is worth the battle. Battles require great energy and spiritual focus.
If we are to emerge victorious, we cannot enter the
battle unprepared. We need a strategy for victory.

Why do we need a strategy? Our strategy begins
with understanding what kind of warrior we are.
Paul categorized mankind into three groups: natural, carnal and spiritual.

Paul writes:

> The natural man does not receive the things of the Spirit of God, for they are foolishness to him...But he who is spiritual judges all things...And I, brethren, could not speak to you as to spiritual people but as to carnal, as to babes in Christ.
>
> —1 Corinthians 2:14–15; 3:1

God doesn't want you merely to set aside *times of worship* as a part of your life. He desires for *your entire life to become worship to Him.*

Although the Corinthians were Christians, they were not fully spiritual; they did not live in full obedience to the Spirit. Neither were they mere natural men, people who did not know Christ. Rather they were carnal Christians who still lived in envy and divisions like the unsaved.[2]

**Natural man**

*Natural man* has been separated from God as a result of Adam's sin. Natural man cannot worship God because he has no relationship with God. He worships, but he does not worship God. We were all created to worship. Some worship jobs, sports figures, money, entertainment, TV personalities or something else. To the natural man, God is the "man upstairs," but there is no personal relationship with Him.

**Carnal man**

*Carnal man* has been redeemed from eternal death by believing in the blood of Jesus. The Holy

Spirit has come to live in him, but his flesh, body and soul (mind, will or emotions) rule him. Carnal man cannot experience true worship because he's caught up with the things of this world. His relationship with God is just part of his life. Carnal man has divided up the pie of his life into specific slices of varying sizes. One slice is work. For many, that's the biggest slice. Another slice may be marriage and family. Another slice could be leisure, hobbies or recreation. Still another slice is church and worship.

For the carnal man, worship is something he does—not something he is. Worship is a small slice of life. Worship has a place in life, but it's not life. So the carnal man worships in services and at church, but he never finds himself worshiping at home with his family or at work as he toils to earn a living. So, the carnal man views worship as a necessary duty usually fulfilled in an hour or two on Sunday.

Ask the carnal man, "Have you worshiped this week?" His response is, "Oh yes, I went to church Sunday morning."

### Spiritual man

Ask the spiritual man, "Have you worshiped this week?" The response will be quite different from the carnal man's answer. The spiritual man will say, "My week has been worship." So who is this *spiritual man?* Spiritual man submits himself completely to the Holy Spirit. He is a man who is led by the Spirit of God.

The spiritual man can worship without ceasing because he has yielded all of his life to the Holy Spirit's leading. The spiritual man is communing as a son with the Father in everything he does and says. "And because you are sons, God has sent forth the Spirit of His Son into your hearts, crying out, 'Abba, Father!'" (Gal. 4:6). His desire to worship the Father is as intense on Monday morning as on Sunday. He worships God just as passionately on the job and at home as in a church service. Instead of part of his life being worship, the spiritual man finds that all of his life is worship.

Within the spiritual man God has deposited the desire to worship Him all the time, in every place and during every situation.

The carnal man, because he does not walk in the Spirit, is always tripping over obstacles and gets ensnared in pitfalls.

> "If it had not been the LORD who was on our
>     side,"
> Let Israel now say—
> "If it had not been the LORD who was on our
>     side,
> When men rose up against us,
> Then they would have swallowed us alive,
> When their wrath was kindled against us;
> Then the waters would have overwhelmed us,
> The stream would have gone over our soul;
> Then the swollen waters
> Would have gone over our soul."
>
> *Blessed be the LORD,*
> *Who has not given us as prey to their teeth.*
> *Our soul has escaped as a bird from the snare of*
> *    the fowlers;*
> *The snare is broken, and we have escaped.*
> Our help is in the name of the LORD,
> Who made heaven and earth.
>                    —PSALM 124:1–8, EMPHASIS ADDED

When the enemy sets a trap, God gives us a way out. How does a bird escape when the snare is broken? The bird (our soul) escapes by spreading its wings and taking flight into the sky. As the spiritual man worships and praises God in all life, he continually escapes the traps and snares of the enemy.

# The spiritual man is communing as a son with the Father in everything he does and says.

If you have ever flown on an airplane, you will understand what I am trying to say. My kids love it when I am able to take them with me on a trip. When we arrive at the gate, they cannot wait to get on the plane. They ask, "Daddy, when are we going to take off?" They don't care anything about the taxi out to the runway—they want to take off! When the plane gets to the runway where it stops and the engines begin to roar, their faces fill with excitement as they say, "Daddy, make sure you are buckled up because we are going to take off now!"

The thrust of the plane is like praise. Worshipful praise is what gets you up and flying. As the pilot increases the thrust, the plane begins to fly higher and higher. Praise gets you out of the clouds…above the turbulence below. Once a plane reaches cruising altitude, the seat belt light goes off, and you are free to move around the cabin. Why can you move around freely now? Because the higher you go, the less resistance and turbulence you encounter.

# The Enemy Sets Traps to Ground Our Praise

The spiritual man must be aware of the wiles and devices of the enemy. As the spiritual man worships in all of life, he will encounter the traps and snares of Satan. Paul warns us to be aware of the enemies devices, "lest Satan should take advantage of us; for we are not ignorant of his devices" (2 Cor. 2:11).

What are the traps that the enemy sets to hinder our worship, ground our praise and distract us from loving God completely and passionately? Let's take a closer look at these traps.

### The trap of pride

Pride completely hinders and will stop true praise and worship. Pride is by far our greatest stumbling block to worship. Pride is a subtle thing and will rear its ugly head when we least expect it. If you are not careful, you can even become proud of your humility.

Being proud of our gifts will lead to a showy display in order to impress others and reveal a secret craving for applause. I have learned much from observing others in the ministry. For example, I have been in some churches where the people worshiped their own worship of God—instead of worshiping God Himself.

Before his exile, Lucifer led worship in heaven. He walked closest to the throne of God until he became prideful and wanted to take God's place.

> You were the anointed cherub who covers;
> I established you;
> You were on the holy mountain of God;

You walked back and forth in the midst of
    fiery stones.
You were perfect in your ways from the day
    you were created,
Till iniquity was found in you.

                      —EZEKIEL 28:14–15

We must be aware of the following facts:

- "Pride goes before destruction, and a haughty spirit before a fall" (Prov. 16:18).

- Pride is a trap. Once it is tripped, it will surely snare its prey. Pride is what led to Lucifer's rebellion against God and to his own demise.

How you are fallen from heaven,
O Lucifer, son of the morning!
How you are cut down to the ground,
You who weakened the nations!
For you have said in your heart:
"I will ascend into heaven,
I will exalt my throne above the stars of God;
I will also sit on the mount of the congrega-
    tion
On the farthest sides of the north;
I will ascend above the heights of the clouds,
I will be like the Most High."

                      —ISAIAH 14:12–14

## The trap of self-will

The ugly twin of pride is *self-will.* Lucifer showed himself in the five *I wills* of Isaiah 14:13–14: "*I will* ascend into heaven. *I will* exalt my throne above the stars of God. *I will* also sit on the mount of the con-gregation. *I will* also ascend above the heights of the clouds. *I will* be like the Most High."

Don't practice these *I wills.* Your *pride* and *self-will* will result in a fall. And now, ladies and gentlemen, fix your eyes on the center ring for the great finale—*the fall*:

> Yet you shall be brought down to Sheol,
> To the lowest depths of the Pit.
>
> —ISAIAH 14:15

One of the saddest stories in the Word of God that deals with self-will is the story of Aaron's two sons, Nadab and Abihu. (See Leviticus 7–10.) In Leviticus we read that God spoke to Moses about anointing Aaron and his sons for the ministry. Moses did everything just as the Lord commanded him. During the preparation for the anointing of Aaron and his sons, the boys went through some pretty intense ceremonies:

> "And you shall not go outside the door of the tabernacle of meeting for seven days, until the days of your consecration are ended. For seven days he shall consecrate you. As he has done this day, so the LORD has commanded to do, to make atonement for you. Therefore you shall stay at the door of the tabernacle of meeting day and night for seven days, and keep the charge of the LORD, so that you may not die; for so I have been commanded." So Aaron and his sons did all the things that the LORD had commanded by the hand of Moses.
>
> —LEVITICUS 8:33–36

They completed seven days of preparation and expectation as they waited for the big day. On the eighth day, Moses called Aaron and his sons and the elders of Israel together (Lev. 9:1).

*The big day when the glory of the Lord was going to appear had arrived.* Then Moses said, "This is the thing which the Lord commanded you to do, and the glory of the Lord will appear to you" (Lev. 9:6).

> Then Aaron lifted his hand toward the people, blessed them, and came down from offering the sin offering, the burnt offering, and peace offerings. And Moses and Aaron went into the tabernacle of meeting, and came out and blessed the people. Then the glory of the LORD appeared to all the people, and fire came out from before the LORD and consumed the burnt offering and the fat on the altar. When all the people saw it, they shouted and fell on their faces.
>
> —LEVITICUS 9:22–24

As consecrated priests to the Lord, Aaron and his sons could serve only in the holy place. They had met all the requirements and were now ready to celebrate. Moses, Aaron, his sons and the people were shouting and rejoicing over the glory of God that they had just witnessed.

## Pride is by far our greatest stumbling block to worship.

Then the unthinkable happened!

> Then Nadab and Abihu, the sons of Aaron, each took his censer and put fire in it, put incense on it, and offered profane fire before the LORD, which He had not commanded them. So fire went out from the LORD and devoured them, and they died before the

LORD. And Moses said to Aaron, "This is what the LORD spoke, saying: 'By those who come near Me, I must be regarded as holy; and before all the people, I must be glorified.' So Aaron held his peace.

—LEVITICUS 10:1–3

In a matter of a few minutes the scene changes; the shouting turns to utter chaos and cries of pain. The first fire brought with it joy. The second brought the judgment of God. The first fire from heaven consumed Aaron's sacrifice. The second fire consumed his two boys.

Rebellious pride costs dearly!

You may be thinking, *What's the big deal? So what; they just added some incense. Is that so bad? Is it worthy of death?*

Nadab and Abihu knew the rules. They knew the commandments of God regarding proper worship. Yet they willingly disobeyed. As a result, they paid a very heavy price—death!

Worship must have its foundation and instruction in the Word of God. The "profane fire" of self-will is not going to go unpunished in the presence of God. We must realize that no person can worship God as he pleases. We have to come to God on His terms—not ours!

### The trap of tradition

Jesus spoke to the religious leaders of His day by saying to them, "[You are] making the word of God of no effect through your tradition which you have handed down. And many such things you do" (Mark 7:13).

Man invented religion to keep God at a safe distance. Humans substituted *religion* for *relationship* with God. They reasoned, "Here's what we will do. We will build God a house and put Him in it. If God stays in the house we build for Him, then we can keep Him out of ours. We will also give God a day of worship (like Sunday), and the other six will be ours to do what we want. We will give Him an hour; that way all the other hours are ours to enjoy. If we keep God at a safe distance, maybe than He won't interfere with what we want to do."

Traditions are those things we do because they have been handed down. Man-taught principles that are not rooted in the Word of God are the traditions of men. A man-made tradition teaches people ways of approaching God religiously, ways that appear to be worship of God in a church setting. But man-made worship is merely lip service— and often the people's hearts are far from Him.

Traditions prompt us to expect things that are irrelevant to God's kingdom. Human tradition expects people to dress and act a certain way at church. We expect worship to last a prescribed length of time. Religion says that we *praise* for a certain length of time, and then we worship. After *worship* we must have announcements. Then we have a message. Tradition says that a certain style must govern the way we sing our songs.

Human traditions dictate the way we worship. But worship isn't prescribed by tradition; it springs from the heart and is led by the Spirit.

In the Old Testament, the Israelites were constantly trying to worship God through tradition instead of from the heart. Listen to what God says through the prophet Micah:

> "How can we make up to you for what we've done?" you ask. "Shall we bow before the Lord with offerings of yearling calves?" Oh no! For if you offered him thousands of rams and ten thousands of rivers of olive oil— would that please him? Would he be satisfied? If you sacrificed your oldest child, would that make him glad? Then would he forgive your sins? Of course not!
>
> —MICAH 6:6–7, TLB

In Job we read that nothing we do moves God:

> If you sin, does that shake the heavens and knock God from his throne? Even if you sin again and again, what effect will it have upon him? Or if you are good, is this some great gift to him? Your sins may hurt another man, or your good deeds may profit him.
>
> —JOB 35:6–8, TLB

Traditions—no matter how good or bad, old or new, exciting or dull—cannot shape true worship. *Traditions* are those things that lessen true worship and cause our faith in God to stifle. They are nothing more than *formalism*, the outward demonstrations of religion, the observance of forms, rules, methods taught by men, that make the Word of God of no effect.

True worship flows from clean hands and a pure heart. In Isaiah 29:13, God reveals:

> Therefore the LORD said:
> "Inasmuch as these people draw near with

their mouths
And honor Me with their lips,
But have removed their hearts far from Me,
And their fear toward Me is taught by the
commandment of men…"

—ISAIAH 29:13

Traditions are formed by the commandments of men. The result of man-made worship takes the shape of an external form shaped by rules, but it doesn't flow out of the inner person, the spirit man—*the heart.*

# Worship isn't prescribed by tradition; it springs from the heart and is led by the Spirit.

A description of spiritual worship is found in John 4:24: "God is Spirit, and those who worship Him *must* worship in spirit and truth" (emphasis added).

## The trap of judgment

Tradition brings along his friend judgment!

You, therefore, have no excuse, you who pass judgment on someone else, for at whatever point you judge the other, you are condemning yourself, because you who pass judgment do the same things.

—ROMANS 2:1, NIV

Those adhering to one tradition quickly judge and condemn those of another tradition. Judgmental people continually immerse those "not like themselves" in bad news. They continually tell others what's wrong with them and with their worship. But worship isn't about focusing on bad news;

it's about the good news of Jesus Christ.

Let's return to the good news of worship. The body of Christ today is experiencing some of the greatest praise and worship music ever. For me, some of the most anointed worship I have ever heard is coming out of Australia. The Lord is using Darlene Zschech (whom I have never met, so it's not a personal plug, but still the truth) and that incredible team around her to touch my life and others around the world.

In every nation where God has allowed me to minister I have had the wonderful privilege of hearing worshipers use songs from Darlene's ministry. These songs have touched my life, and I am seeing how they are touching the body of Christ everywhere. But anointed songs are not the test of true worship. If we try to make these songs—or any others—the test of true worship, they will become the tools of tradition instead of the instruments of praise and worship they were intended to be.

Even great worshiping churches fall into the traps called *tradition* and *judgment*. They start out worshiping from the heart, but after awhile they end up worshiping their own worship—and not worshiping God.

The trap of judgment can easily lead us into the next trap—a critical spirit.

## The trap of a critical spirit

A critical spirit can really sour the sweet spirit of worship. What is a critical spirit? It is the negative habit of finding fault with everything and everyone. Beyond a doubt, it will devastate worship. When we criticize rather than correct and encourage, we not only condemn the person we are criticizing, but we also condemn ourselves. The enemy loves it when people are critical because the trap of a critical spirit will keep a person from becoming a true worshiper. When we judge, condemn and criticize others, we build a wall that separates us from the presence of God.

We need to remember to keep our eyes on Jesus, who is perfect, because man is not. We will always be able to find something we don't like about others. In Isaiah 58, the Lord speaks pointedly about our tendency to criticize others by saying:

> Then you shall call, and the LORD will answer;
> You shall cry, and He will say, "Here I am."
>
> *If you take away the yoke from your midst,*
> *The pointing of the finger, and speaking*
>     *wickedness…*
> Then your light shall dawn in the darkness,
> And your darkness shall be as the noonday.
>                 —ISAIAH 58:9–10, EMPHASIS ADDED

Here's what happens with a critical spirit. As long as we are pointing out the weaknesses of others, we don't have time to allow God to cleanse us from our own. And that keeps us from entering His presence!

People with a critical spirit can easily point out the faults in others because they often struggle with the same trouble themselves. People with critical spirits will always major on minor issues. Everything is distorted because they haven't gotten their own eyes or heart checked. They demand a standard of holiness from others that they are not prepared to live themselves.

A critic is so intent on removing what he thinks to be a log in his brother's eye that he does not realize the huge plank in his own eye! (See Luke 6:41–42.) For example, what he calls a *bad temper* in others he excuses as *righteous indignation* in his own life.

> ## A critical spirit can really sour the sweet spirit of worship.

Remember that worship is about *good news*, not bad news. Our focus should not be the bad news evident in the lives of others. Our focus should be the good news that all of us are becoming new creations in Christ Jesus.

How can we be freed from this awful faultfinding spirit? John writes:

> If we confess our sins, He is faithful and just to forgive us our sins and to cleanse us from all unrighteousness…My little children, these things I write to you, so that you may not sin. And if anyone sins, we have an Advocate with the Father, Jesus Christ the righteous. And He Himself is the propitiation for our sins, and not for ours only but also for the whole world.
> —1 JOHN 1:9, 2:1–2

Your criticism of another person will not change that person. People are changed in God's presence. Refocus your criticism into prayer. Pray that others will enter God's presence. Pray that you will stay in God's presence so that you too will be changed. Pray that God changes you from criticizing to encouraging…from being judgmental to being discerning…

and from being condemning to being compassion-
ate.

## The trap of ignorance

The enemy wants to keep us in the dark about
worship. He wants to keep us ignorant, trapped in
our own lack of knowledge.

There is a correct and an incorrect way to worship
God. Once we have heard the truth, there is really no
excuse for our ignorance. Lacking the spiritual knowledge to "worship in truth" not only keeps us from true
worship; it can easily lead us into incorrect worship
that has harmful side effects. In Hosea 4:6 we learn,
"My people are destroyed for lack of knowledge."

The ancient Hebrew people considered *knowledge*
to be the active and dynamic entry into an intimate
relationship. For them, to "know" God was to enter
into an intimate relationship with Him.
"Knowledge" (*yada* in Hebrew) is the closest intimacy between two people and the knowledge
acquired from such an intimacy. To be intimate with
God is to know Him with both the head and the
heart. It's an intimacy that develops from *experience*,
not just from education or theory.

So how do I know when I have worshiped Him
correctly? Look for rain! Rain? You may be saying,
"Sam, what are you talking about? What does rain
have to do with worshiping God?" Well, I'm glad
you asked. Consider what God says about true worship and rain:

> And it shall be that if you earnestly obey My
> commandments which I command you today,
> to love the LORD your God and serve Him with

all your heart and with all your soul, then I
will give you the rain for your land in its season, the early rain and the latter rain, that you
may gather in your grain, your new wine, and
your oil.

—DEUTERONOMY 11:13–14

And it shall be that whichever of the families
of the earth do not come up to Jerusalem to
worship the King, the LORD of hosts, on them
there will be no rain.

—ZECHARIAH 14:17

When you are worshiping God, do the heavens
above you seem opened, or are they closed? Rain
heralds the presence of God in our midst. No rain is
an indicator that God's presence is not getting
through our man-made walls and hindrances!

Do any of the worthless idols of the nations
bring rain?
Do the skies themselves send down showers?
No, it is you, O LORD our God.
Therefore our hope is in you,
for you are the one who does all this.

—JEREMIAH 14:22, NIV

In the past, out of ignorance we may have worshiped all the wrong gods. But through knowledge of
the living God, we now worship Him and receive rain
from heaven to water us, sustain us and make us
fruitful.

## The trap of a religious spirit

You may not have fallen into this trap, but I want
you to be aware of how to minister to someone who
has been snared by religion. Let me explain my

interpretation of someone who has a religious spirit. A religious spirit manifests itself as "having a form of godliness but denying its power" (2 Tim. 3:5). A person with a religious spirit is one who refuses to have the fullness of God in his or her life. A religious person wants to control God instead of surrendering all control to God.

When it comes to your relationship with God, do you find yourself doing more and worshiping less? If worship is attached to *where* you worship, and not to *whom* you worship, you may be about to fall into the religious trap.

## A religious person wants to control God instead of surrendering all control to God.

Jesus addressed a religious spirit in the Samaritan woman by explaining to her that worship is not the result of *where* she worshiped; it comes as the result of *whom* she worshiped:

> "Our fathers worshiped on this mountain, and you Jews say that in Jerusalem is the place *where one ought to worship.*" Jesus said to her, "Woman, believe Me, the hour is coming when you will neither on this mountain, nor in Jerusalem, worship the Father."
> —JOHN 4:20–21, EMPHASIS ADDED

Because Judah became religious instead of staying intimate with God, she found herself in Babylonian exile. From the place of their captivity, the Israelites sang:

By the rivers of Babylon,
There we sat down, yea, we wept.
When we remembered Zion:
We hung our harps
Upon the willows in the midst of it.
For there those who carried us away captive
        asked of us a song,
And those who plundered us requested mirth,
Saying, "Sing us one of the songs of Zion!"

How shall we sing the LORD's song
In a foreign land?

—PSALM 137:1–4

Why were the people in Babylon instead of Zion where they should have been? They were dwelling in a land of false religion instead of dwelling in Zion where they were able to worship the true God. They had become ensnared by a religious spirit, and it had resulted in their captivity in a foreign land.

Be careful of the company you keep. Religious people will not only affect your worship—they may also infect you. It is not only the world where you may encounter someone with a religious spirit— they may be sitting next to you in the pew at church. If I had to make a choice between hanging out with someone who is not saved but who needs Jesus or someone who is really religious, I would choose to spend time with the unsaved seeker. At least the heathen knows that he needs God. The religious person is deceived into thinking that he has found God when all he has truly found is false religion.

True worship will set us free from the bondage of twisted belief and a fake religious system. Only as we truly worship God is our spirit released from captivity to soar into the presence of God.

There is a place where only a few have walked. It's been reserved for a special group of people called the *true worshipers of God.* "That path no bird knows, nor has the falcon's eye seen it. The proud lions have not trodden it, nor has the fierce lion passed over it" (Job 28:7–8). True worshipers seek a relationship with God—not a religious system that claims to know about Him. No religious system… no religious spirit has ever personally or intimately kissed the face of God.

> True worshipers seek a relationship with God—not a religious system that claims to know about Him.

### The trap of unforgiveness

Holding unforgiveness against anyone, whether the offense is real or imagined, hinders worship. If we are going to enter into God's presence, forgiveness is a must. We shouldn't even partake of the Lord's table if we have unforgiveness in our hearts. Forgiveness is an iniquity that separates us from God:

> Behold, the LORD's hand is not shortened,
> That it cannot save;
> Nor His ear heavy,
> That it cannot hear.
> But your iniquities have separated you from
>     your God;
> And your sins have hidden His face from you,
> So that He will not hear.
>
> —ISAIAH 59:1–2

Forgiveness is not optional for the true worshiper. Forgiveness is a requirement. God won't forgive us if we refuse to forgive others for their offense. The Lord makes this clear in the Sermon on the Mount when He says, "And forgive us our debts, as we forgive our debtors...For if you forgive men their trespasses, your heavenly Father will also forgive you. But if you do not forgive men their trespasses, neither will your Father forgive your trespasses" (Matt. 6:12, 14–15).

How do we really forgive someone who has wronged us? In both the Old and New Testaments, God states repeatedly that the only way to come into the presence of God is with a heart free from sin. Until we choose to forgive everyone of every wrong against us, worship will be impossible. "And when you stand praying, if you hold anything against anyone, forgive him, so that your Father in heaven may forgive you your sins" (Mark 11:25, NIV).

What is biblical forgiveness? Forgiveness lets go of the pain, hurt and feelings of revenge. Genuine forgiveness wills to forgive even if the other person doesn't repent. Proverbs helps us understand authentic forgiveness.

> A man's wisdom gives him patience; it is to his glory to overlook an offense.
> —PROVERBS 19:11, NIV

> Do not say, "I'll do to him as he has done to me; I'll pay that man back for what he did."
> —PROVERBS 24:29, NIV

Jesus declares the necessity of forgiveness: "For if you forgive men when they sin against you, your heavenly Father will also forgive you" (Matt. 6:14, NIV). Forgiveness is the act of excusing or pardoning another in spite of his shortcomings and mistakes. Biblical forgiveness demands us to forgive others, because God's grace brings responsibility and obligation. We are under an obligation to forgive because God has forgiven us:

> But God demonstrates his own love for us in this: While we were still sinners, Christ died for us. Since we have now been justified by his blood, how much more shall we be saved from God's wrath through him!
>
> —ROMANS 5:8–9, NIV

By the way, Jesus placed no limits on the extent to which Christians are to forgive. When we have a forgiving spirit, it really shows that we are true followers of Jesus Christ.

I am asking you to please examine your own heart for places where you may have become trapped by unforgiveness. God wants to break those strongholds in your life.

## The complaining trap

Complaining became the daily habit among the children of Israel as they trekked across the wilderness. Their complaining attacked the spiritual leaders who were leading them to God's presence at Mt. Sinai.

> Then the whole congregation of the children of Israel complained against Moses and Aaron in the wilderness. And the children of Israel said to them, "Oh, that we had died by the hand of the LORD in the land of Egypt, when we sat by the pots of meat and when we ate

bread to the full! For you have brought us out into this wilderness to kill this whole assembly with hunger."

—EXODUS 16:2–3

Moses—and God through Moses—rebuked the people for their complaining. But the complaining continued. Their complaints invoked the wrath of God on a number of occasions, bringing misery and God's judgment against Israel. "Now when the people complained, it displeased the LORD; for the LORD heard it, and His anger was aroused. So the fire of the LORD burned among them, and consumed some in the outskirts of the camp" (Num. 11:1).

Complaining always provokes God's wrath. Complaining constructs a wall of doubt and mistrust between us and the presence of God. Complaining always focuses on a problem or a person *instead of on Jesus.* When we complain about music, music can no longer help focus us on God's presence. When we complain about the message, the message can no longer minister God's Word to us. When we complain about the pastor, the pastor can no longer help to nurture us with God's comforting touch. Complaining cuts us off from the power of God's presence to touch us, teach us, fill us or change us.

Take your eyes off the problem or people and fix your eyes on Jesus. Stop complaining and start worshiping. When you focus on the way you worship, you will always be able to find something to complain about. But when you kiss God's face, your only thought will be, *O, how I love Jesus!*

**The gossiping trap**

So many traps and snares exist and are used by the enemy to distract us from true worship. I have neither time nor space to highlight all of them, but one more deserves our attention now—gossip. Gossip passes on something about another person that will hurt or harm that person. Gossip abandons speaking the truth in love. Instead, gossips speak whatever they hear, never caring whom they hurt or what the truth is.

Scripture reveals that, "A gossip betrays a confidence; so avoid a man who talks too much" (Prov. 20:19, NIV). When a juicy morsel surfaces in the church, all the gossips seem to find one another really quickly. Not only does gossip hurt others, but it also distracts one's heart from true worship. In the midst of what should be worship to God, the entrapped gossiper is thinking about what he or she has just heard about another person instead of thinking about what God has just said.

If a gossiper comes to you before, during or after worship, act quickly and assertively. Take the gossiper directly to the person about whom the other person is speaking. Let the gossiper speak face to face to the person they are libeling. The lips of a gossiper are filled with lies, deceit and malice. No lips that gossip can kiss the face of God.

# Get Out of the Traps!

Is your soul in prison? Has the enemy been at war with you? Are you in captivity? Were you once free and now in bondage? Are you battling a religious spirit? Are you with the wrong crowd? Are you bound up with traditions? Have you made judgments against others? Has pride completely hindered you? Do you have a critical spirit? Most importantly, are you holding on to unforgiveness in your heart? Are you gossiping or listening to gossip?

These are but a few of the things that will interrupt the flow of the Holy Spirit in your life. Jesus died on the cross and took your sins with Him. Our only hope lies in who Jesus is and what He did for us.

> Is your deepest desire to kiss the face of God with true worship?

Friend, on the cross of Jesus, the wrath of God and the love of God came together for you. He took the wrath of God upon Himself because He loves you. He took the punishment for your sins to satisfy the justice of God. Jesus died to set you free from sin and free to worship. Jesus died to set you free from every snare and trap of the enemy.

Is your deepest desire to kiss the face of God with true worship? If so, take these important steps:

## To Kiss God's Face…

1. Confess any hindrance that builds a wall between you and the living God.

2. Ask God's presence to make you more receptive to His changes in your life.

3. Humble yourself before God and others.

4. Shun man-made traditions.

5. Replace criticism with encouragement.

6. Repent of unforgiveness, and determine always to forgive others—even if they don't repent and ask for forgiveness!

7. Stop complaining; start praising.

8. Refuse to listen to gossip or to pass on gossip.

9. Pray this: *Lord Jesus, deliver me from every trap or snare of the enemy. Thank You for dying for me to set me free to worship You in spirit and truth. Amen.*

# Chapter 3

## *Simply* Falling *in* Love *With* Jesus

A s I began writing this chapter, I was
reminded about how important it is to tell
Jesus just how much I love Him. As I have
learned about worship throughout my life, God has
always used my children to teach me the valuable
lessons of simplicity.

On a recent morning, God reminded me of the
need for simplicity in worship when my youngest
child, Christa, came into our bedroom early in the
morning, as she often does. She simply stood by
our bed and waited to see if her mom or dad would
stir. As soon as she saw us look at her through
sleepy, half-opened eyes, she leaned over and gave
us a big morning kiss. Then she jumped up into the
bed with us and just snuggled for a few minutes.
Soon, she jumped up and wanted breakfast. That
brief time with us was so nice—while it lasted!

Through that incident, the Lord reminded me
about how complicated my worship had become. I
was convicted about how long it had been since

I simply blew Him a kiss and said, "Jesus, I love You." Just as Christa's first desire in the morning was to kiss her parents and spend time snuggling with them, so our desire in worship should be simply this: *kissing God's face and spending time with Him.*

Permit me to explain. When my children were younger, every night before they went to sleep we prayed together. At the end of our prayer time I would say, "Let's give Jesus a big kiss." They blew Jesus a big kiss and told Him that they loved Him. What did this teach them? It taught them that worship, to be true worship, must be an expression of love.

Blowing Jesus a kiss became very big in my family. This expression of worship eventually became one of things that I loved doing in all the worship services that I led. I just wanted people to understand how simple worship can be and how complicated we have made it.

One night after praying with Christa as she went to bed, we both blew Jesus a big kiss. As I turned to walk out of her room, Christa said, "Daddy, blow me a kiss." So I did.

Then she did something that has left a mark on my life. Christa taught me just how simple worship can be. As I blew her a kiss, she threw her hand into the air as if to catch it out of midair. Then she kissed my imaginary kiss and ate it, enabling my kiss—my love—to go down deep into her heart.

It just sounds too simple, doesn't it? I don't know about you, but right now my heart is pounding with conviction: "Lord Jesus, bring back the simplicity of worship into my own heart. I've learned to complicate what can be so simple." I wonder how many mornings have gone by when He just stood there staring at us, waiting for any kind of movement. God patiently comes to us and waits. God anticipates our awakening so that we will tell Him, "I love You." God waits for us to kiss His face.

## A Journey Toward True Worship

Over the past seventeen years, I've been on a journey to learn all that I can about what true worship really is. The years have been filled with teachings, studies and listening to others teach about worship. I have traveled to conferences where the whole conference program was developed to learn about worship and what it means.

> Never lose the simplicity of just falling in love with Jesus and simply blowing Him a big kiss.

There are many wonderful "schools of worship" all over the world. People everywhere have a genuine personal hunger to learn all that they can about worship. People have made every attempt to describe what it is and how to do it right. Volumes of books have been written on nothing else but worship.

Go to the conferences. Read the books. Take volumes of notes. Listen to tapes and CDs. But please, never lose the simplicity of just falling in love with Jesus and simply blowing Him a big kiss. It sounds too simple—almost foolish—but do it anyway. Why not? You've tried everything else.

Come on; I dare you to put this book down and do something that may feel foolish at first. Put your hand on your mouth and just do it: Blow Him a big kiss. Then tell Jesus how much you love Him. Now, if you dared to do that just now, wasn't it simple, almost too simple? I truly believe that a simple act of blowing a kiss to Jesus, done with all your heart, can be as effective as standing for hours in a service singing your favorite worship songs.

As I mentioned earlier in this book, I believe that many in the body of Christ are living in days of genuine personal hunger after God like never before. I am so hungry for more of God in my life that words are so inadequate. I am not satisfied with living in the memories of my past experiences of knowing Him. *There must be more!* So what is it?

## Simply Put, Worship Is Loving Jesus

True worship is almost impossible to explain or define. The purpose of this book is *not* to define worship, because I can't. It's my deepest prayer that God will take this simple book, which contains the past seventeen years of my journey in worship, and use it as a blessing for you. I pray for God to use me in your life even though we may have never met. Even as I write I am praying that God will create an insatiable hunger in your heart for Him. I want this book to encourage you to fall in love with Jesus all over again.

Someone once asked me, "How would you define worship?"

My response to him was, "How would you define

love?" What is love? Love is something that happens in your heart and grows daily for that special someone in your life.

Love isn't a step-by-step process; it's a deepening well in our hearts. Love is a spontaneous action. Love can be best described as a verb instead of a noun. Love acts. In much the same way, worship cannot be defined in words. Instead, it's a spontaneous expression to the One our heart loves deeply.

Worship is *all* about Jesus. God doesn't seek your worship; He seeks you. God searches for true worshipers. Worship starts with God's love. As we receive His love for us, we then respond to that love. We do not earn or prompt God's love; we respond to it. When we become aware of God's love, then we respond to Him with our worship, which really is our life.

Let me show you what I mean. In John 3:16 we read a very familiar verse about God's love for us. Worship begins with understanding that "God so loved the world that He gave His only begotten Son, that whoever believes in Him should not perish but have everlasting life."

> ### God doesn't seek your worship; He seeks you.

In 1 John 4:9–10 we read:

> In this the love of God was manifested toward us, that God has sent His only begotten Son into the world, that we might live through Him. In this is love, not that we loved God, but that He loved us and sent His Son to be the propitiation for our sins.

If worship and the lifestyle of worship are not built on a solid foundation, our Christian walk will be like riding a roller coaster. One day we are up and flying high and screaming about how good God is. Then before we know it, we're on the top looking down that first huge plunge, crying, "O God, where are You?"

Why does this happen to so many believers? I believe it's because we have insulted God by demeaning the precious gift of worship that He has given us. In the church, worship has become a time filler in a service rather than a lifestyle.

## You Are Created to Worship

Worship is not something you do; worship is who God created you to be. God is after you—not your worship songs. God doesn't need your songs. He wants you to be the song. He wants you to be the worship. Worship is a lifestyle rather than a time in service on Sunday or Wednesday.

I have passed hundreds of church marquees inviting everyone, "Come and worship." People come, but all they really do is hear a message. They come, but they never worship. I have seen many signs that read, "Morning Worship—11:00 A.M. Evening Worship—6:00 P.M."

So, what's the problem? Why don't more believers understand what true worship really is? Why are so many people still experiencing such a hunger within for the presence of God?

The problem is a mind-set. Of course, having worship services is not the problem. But too many

Christians have the paradigm that worship happens at a place—a building called *church*, and it happens during a certain time—on Sundays. Worship isn't a service, just as church isn't a building. Worship is a lifestyle. Church is a person. Say aloud to yourself, "I am the church. My life is the worship service."

Worship must be more than merely a time filler between the collection of the offering and the sermon. There is nothing wrong with an order of service for our Sunday services. But what if God wants to interrupt our plan with His plan? What if He supercedes our order of service with a move of His Spirit? Would He have our permission to do it?

> Worship is a lifestyle.
> Church is a person.

In some services the remarks before the offering have been longer than the period of time allowed for people to express their hearts to God. Sadly, when hearts are being touched the most, we often stop the worship to say, "And now if you will please look in your bulletin for some very important announcements." Have we become so blind to the Spirit of God that we think that a good message can replace the presence of God in worship?

I hear people all over the body of Christ crying out, "There must be more to God…right?"

You see, it's not just others who are asking for more. I am asking, "This can't be it, can it? There must be more to God, right?"

The answer is a wholehearted, YES! There is more for us to experience in worshiping God. Yes, there is more than what we have already tasted! It is my deepest desire to see God's people *become* worship rather than *have* a time of worship.

## God Seeks True Worshipers

In the Old Covenant, it was the worshiper who sought God. But in the New Covenant it is God who seeks the worshiper.

> But the hour is coming, and now is, when the true worshipers will worship the Father in spirit and truth; *for the Father is seeking such to worship Him.*
>
> —JOHN 4:23, EMPHASIS ADDED

What a thought! In this present age, it's God the Father who is seeking us. The purpose of the Father is to seek such to worship Him in spirit and truth. He is not after your worship, but through worship He gets what He wants—you!

Just as the purpose of the Father is to seek true worshipers, the purpose of Jesus coming into this world was declared in Luke 19:10: "For the Son of man is come to seek and to save that which was lost" (KJV).

In Ezekiel 34:16, God declared, "I will seek what was lost and bring back what was driven away, bind up the broken and strengthen what was sick; but I will destroy the fat and the strong, and feed them in judgment." This was the search that led Jesus all the way to the cross. In the same way, it is the Father's purpose to seek out true worshipers who will worship Him in spirit and truth.

Stop the presses. "Selah!" Think. Meditate on this

for a long while. God…the Father…the high and lofty One who inhabits eternity…is not just *looking* for you—He *wants* you!

Now let me bring it all home. What is the cause of many unfilled dreams and blessings? Why are so many hearts still empty and broken? What is the cause of countless broken hearts in ministry? Look at what worship has become, whether out of ignorance or just plain disobedience to a loving God who wants to do more in us then we have ever dreamed.

The psalms declare, "*Give* unto the Lord the glory due to His name; *worship* the Lord in the beauty of holiness" (Ps. 29:2, emphasis added). The prophet declares, "Will a man rob [defraud] God? Yet you have robbed Me! But you say, *'In what way have we robbed You?'*" (Mal. 3:8, emphasis added). The deep truth of this revelation rings loud in the church today. In the same way that Israel robbed God in tithes and offerings, for one reason or another many are defrauding Him of what matters most. They are withholding from God what He seeks and rightfully deserves. *Worship*!

What have we done? Have we come so low as to bite off the hand that feeds us? Do we actually think that we will get away with this kind of robbery? Will man, whose life depends on God and who receives all things from Him, now rob Him?

We ask, "God, what do You mean? How have we robbed You? What are You talking about? In what way have we robbed You? We have done nothing wrong!" Learn this life lesson: People with a wrong motivation of heart will always blame others for the condition of their own hearts. Those who are guilty of robbing Him are not willing to confess their guilt. They rob God and then act as if they don't know what He's talking about. They have robbed Him of honor. They have robbed Him of devotion. They have robbed Him of themselves, and yet they have the audacity to ask, "In what way have we robbed You?" People can be easily fooled, but we will never con God.

If we really want to draw closer to God, if our worship is to be acceptable to Him, then worship must take on a godly lifestyle. Worship is about Him. It's about His presence. It's about His love for us. It's about what He wants to do in us and for us. It's about His love capturing us. Then and only then can we offer Him worship in spirit and truth.

God desires wholehearted worship. He doesn't want us just to sing *about* Him to Him. He wants us to give our hearts to Him as our worship.

## Worship is only a vehicle to get us into the presence of God.

God has never been impressed with our music or our ability to play an instrument or even with our singing about Him. He wants our *worship*, not our singing. He wants our hearts, not just our nice songs. Merely singing songs from words on transparencies or in PowerPoint presentations cannot express worship on Sunday morning. Sadly, so many substitute their heartfelt worship for "transparency worship." They think that singing other people's songs will satisfy God.

Singing the songs of others should only be an encouragement to express our own heart's song. Worship is only a vehicle to get us into the presence of God. Worship is about His presence coming and touching us as He waits for our response. Worship is about loving God:

> Though I speak with the tongues of men and of angels, but have not love, I have become sounding brass or a clanging cymbal. And though I have the gift of prophecy, and understand all mysteries and all knowledge, and though I have all faith, so that I could remove mountains, but have not love, I am nothing. And though I bestow all my goods to feed the poor, and though I give my body to be burned, but have not love, it profits me nothing.
>
> —1 Corinthians 13:1–3

Worship is expressed in loving God and loving people. Those who love God but don't love people are like an empty wagon on the loose, coming down a big hill. The wagon makes a lot of noise because there is nothing in it.

## "Welcome Into My Presence"

A few years ago I was ministering at a wonderful church in Indiana. During the worship that night, the presence of God began to touch me deeply. I felt the presence of God as my body began to tremble. While we were worshiping God in that service, I said to the Lord, "It's great just to be in Your presence again. Lord, I invite Your presence in this place."

The Lord spoke to my heart and said, "No, Sam,

I invite you into My presence. I welcome you into My presence."

The highest priority of worship is that He invites us into His presence, not that we invite Him into ours. We read of God's invitation in Exodus 24:12 (emphasis added):

> Then the LORD said to Moses, "*Come up to Me* on the mountain and be there; and I will give you tablets of stone, and the law and commandments which I have written, that you may teach them."

In Revelation 4:1, God again invites us into His presence (emphasis added):

> After these things I looked, and behold, a door standing open in heaven. And the first voice which I heard was like a trumpet speaking with me, saying, "*Come up here, and I will show you things* which must take place after this."

Worship brings us into fellowship with God, and fellowship will bring revelation. God touches you with His presence because He desires to have fellowship with you.

## The highest priority of worship is that He invites us into His presence, not that we invite Him into ours.

God is not after your worship; He wants to have fellowship with you. Worship will lead you into living in fellowship with Him. But it doesn't end there. He wants fellowship with you because He wants to reveal Himself to you. We don't initiate worship; we simply respond to worship.

## You Were Created to Worship

You were *created* to worship and *called* into ministry. Many people, even some of God's servants, have this reversed. They think they were created to be in the ministry and called to worship. What a mistake this is. We love Him because of *who He is* and not *what He has done for* us.

> ### Ministry is what I do; worship is who I am.

The difference between *worship* and *ministry* is simply this: Ministry is that which comes down to us from the Father through His Son. In the power of the Holy Spirit, one of God's servants flows in the anointing with God's purpose in that specific ministry.

On the other hand, worship is that which goes up from the believer by the Holy Spirit's power, through the Son, to the Father. Ministry descends from God to us. Worship ascends from us to God. *Ministry is what I do; worship is who I am.*

The question is not whether or not you will worship. The issue is whom or what you will worship. You were created to worship, and you will worship something or someone. Some people will worship cars; others will worship sports, money, home or career. Some will even worship preachers. (This is a no-no!)

# What Is Worship in Spirit and Truth?

Jesus declared:

> But the hour is coming, and now is, when the true worshipers *will worship the Father in spirit and truth;* for the Father is seeking such to worship Him.
>
> —JOHN 4:23, EMPHASIS ADDED

You may be wondering, "Is it possible for someone to draw closer to God with just lip service?" God answers that question in Isaiah 29:13:

> Therefore the Lord said: "Inasmuch as these people draw near with their mouths and honor Me with their lips, but have removed their hearts far from Me, and their fear toward Me is taught by the commandment of men..."

How you come into worship is as important as your actual worship. Your spiritual condition is a major factor as to whether or not worship is acceptable. Read what God says through His prophet Ezekiel: "So they come to you as people do, they sit before you as My people, and they hear your words, but they do not do them; for with their mouth they show much love, but their hearts pursue their own gain" (Ezek. 33:31).

We might as well let the Lord's scalpel cut a little deeper and remove anything in our hearts that is not of God. It is possible to sing songs, have great melodies, sing hymns and even express the most beautiful words in worship, and yet fail to reach God's ear and heart. The "worth-ship" of the worship is determined by the sincerity of the worshiper.

**Worship must be in spirit.**

"God is Spirit, and those who worship Him *must worship* in spirit and truth" (John 4:24, emphasis added). Jesus established that this kind of worship was the only acceptable worship. God accepts no other kind. This kind of worship is prompted, led and empowered by the Holy Spirit. Worship in spirit is worship with the Word of God in our hands and the Spirit of God in our hearts.

Notice the order that Jesus emphasized as the right kind of worship. The Father is seeking those who would worship Him in, one, "spirit" and, two, "truth."

> The "worth-ship" of the worship is determined by the sincerity of the worshiper.

The sincerity of worship takes priority over the method of how we worship. The truth is that our worship must not only be guided by the truth of God's Word, but it must also be presented in a truthful and sincere way. Just a gentle reminder: God is looking for *worshipers*, not *worship*.

**God hates hypocrisy.**

*Hypocrisy* is "pretending to be what we don't intend to be." The word *sincere* means "without wax." In today's terminology, "plastic, fake worship makes God sick to His stomach." Sorry for being brutally honest, but then Jesus made some brutally honest statements, like this one: "But go and learn what this means: *'I desire mercy and not sacrifice.'* For

I did not come to call the righteous, but sinners, to repentance" (Matt. 9:13, emphasis added).

God came to abolish all forms of worship that are empty of meaning and life. He was taking down the cover of worship in favor of the heart of worship.

> For I desire mercy [goodness, kindness, faith-fulness], not sacrifice, and acknowledgment of God rather than burnt offerings.
>
> —HOSEA 6:6, NIV

God wants truth—genuine worship from genuine hearts. I wonder what God sees when He looks down from heaven and sees His church. Are we guilty of fake worship? The following verse shows how God views a church that is just a little short on sincerity in worship.

> I hate, I despise your religious feasts; I cannot stand your assemblies. Even though you bring me burnt offerings and grain offerings, I will not accept them. Though you bring choice fel-lowship offerings, I will have no regard for them. Away with the noise of your songs! I will not listen to the music of your harps. But let justice roll on like a river, righteousness like a never-failing stream!
>
> —AMOS 5:21–24, NIV

God looks to see if our lifestyle is backed by our mouth-style. He looks for consistency between the two. It was with this in mind that David said, "Behold, You desire truth in the inward parts" (Ps. 51:6).

If our worship is to be spiritual and sincere, we must allow God to deal with our hearts. All decep-tion, hypocrisy and fake, plastic attitudes must be avoided. Transparent honesty is what He is after. Clean hands and purity of heart bring God delight.

I invite you right now to begin worshiping God in spirit and truth. Let the Holy Spirit empower your worship so that you become worship—overflowing with praise, song, adoration and love. Become transparent in your worship. Let truth reveal your inner self. Rip off the masks and facades so that the true you worships the God of truth. In spirit and truth, your worship will then lead you into His presence as you kiss the face of God.

# To Kiss God's Face...

1. Love Jesus purely and wholeheartedly.

2. Blow a kiss of love to God.

3. Instead of just *going* to worship, *become* worship.

4. Let your whole being become the instruments and the songs of worship.

5. Listen for God's invitation to you, "Come up to Me."

6. Accept ministry as your calling; celebrate worship as your created purpose.

7. Invite the Holy Spirit to empower your worship.

8. Become transparent and utterly truthful in your worship.

# Chapter 4

## Thirsting After Living Water

Worship increases our thirst for living water. So many people come to worship hoping to quench their thirst. But no service, message or music can truly satisfy our deep thirst for the living God.

When I travel, I miss my family terribly. I actually have pictures of my family in my Bible so that I can look at them whenever I want and pray for them. But looking at those pictures never satisfies my desire to be with them. In fact, just the opposite occurs. The pictures of my family increase my thirst and my desire to be with them. Looking at those pictures brings back wonderful memories of the past and the thirst to create new memories with them as soon as I rush back home.

Worship is like that. As we sing familiar hymns and choruses, as we hear God's Word and partake of communion, as we fellowship with God's people, we stir up wonderful memories of God's presence.

Worship evokes the pictures from the past etched eternally on our hearts. We remember the wonderful times we have experienced in God's presence. And we hunger and thirst for more of God.

## Born of Water and the Spirit

We have been born of water. Without it we die, physically and spiritually. Just as a spring of water can refresh us physically, the well of worship can stir up the rivers of living water within us. Jesus taught, "Most assuredly, I say to you, unless one is born of water and the Spirit, he cannot enter the kingdom of God" (John 3:5). The living water that birthed us also flows within us: "But whoever drinks of the water that I shall give him will never thirst. But the water that I shall give him will become in him a fountain of water springing up into everlasting life" (John 4:14).

In John 3, Jesus was talking to a Pharisee named Nicodemus. He was a ruler of the Jews, a moral and upright man who had known the law of God, but now would experience more than the letter of the Law. He would encounter the love of God. I believe this man was hungry for more of God than what the Law taught him.

Jesus opened His heart to this man and said, "Unless one is born of water and the Spirit, he cannot enter the kingdom of God." Water refers to baptism and the repentance from dead works that John the Baptist had emphasized while preaching in the wilderness. Jesus added this very important element in salvation, "...and the Spirit." If Nicodemus thought that salvation came by water alone, he was about to discover that he must be born of the Spirit as well. It's the power and life of the Holy Spirit that changes hearts and gives entrance into the presence of God.

When you were born again and received Jesus as your Savior, this living water filled your inner being. However, it does not spring up as a fountain of living water until you worship. If water has no movement, even good water can become stagnant and go bad. Worship causes water movement in our spirit. The waters that lay still become a fountain springing up into everlasting life when worship occurs. So Jesus affirmed, "But whoever drinks of the water that I shall give him will never thirst. But the water that I shall give him will become *in him a fountain of water springing up* into everlasting life" (John 4:14, emphasis added).

> Therefore with joy you will draw water from the wells of salvation.
>
> —Isaiah 12:3

Wells are not brooks or streams, which can easily dry up because of heat and evaporation. Wells are deep reservoirs underground. The phrase "wells of salvation" refers to an ever-flowing fountain on the inside of you. When it is released, it flows out of you like a river.

In Scripture, we read of only a few times when Jesus offered living water. One example is in John 4 when He offered living water to the woman at the well. In John 7, we find Jesus attending the celebration of the Feast of Tabernacles along with the multitudes of people gathered in Jerusalem. On the last day of the celebration of this feast, the Levitical priests brought water in a golden pitcher from the fountain of Siloam. They mingled wine with the water, and then poured it upon the sacrifice on the altar. Water from as many as eighty pitchers poured over the sacrifice and began to flow down over the temple steps.

On this final, climactic day of the Feast of Tabernacles, Jesus offered water to the thirsty people who had gathered.

> On the last day, that great day of the feast, Jesus stood and cried out, saying, "If anyone thirsts, let him come to Me and drink. He who believes in Me, as the Scripture has said, *out of his heart will flow rivers of living water.*"
> —JOHN 7:37–38, EMPHASIS ADDED

Before living water can flow like a river from the heart, there first must be repentance. "So they gathered together at Mizpah, drew water, and poured it out before the LORD. And they fasted that day, and said there, 'We have sinned against the LORD.' And Samuel judged the children of Israel at Mizpah" (1 Sam. 7:6).

Is there a thirst in your spirit for more of Him? If so, it must begin with repentance from sin. If you are thirsty for more of His presence in your life, it's not enough just to come to Jesus. I remember when I was a kid back in school. During recess or P.E., we would be outside playing, running around doing all sorts of fun stuff, and I would get so thirsty. Imagine me running to the fountain and just standing in front of it. Staring does me no good. Looking at the fountain is not enough, because the purpose is to come and drink.

Coming to Jesus and standing at the altar is a good start, but it will not satisfy the deep thirst for Him inside of you. Being satisfied with just feeling the presence of God around you is not enough. You must drink in His living water. In the words of Jesus, "If anyone thirsts, let him come to Me and drink" (John 7:37).

Standing in front of the fountain cannot and will not satisfy your longing. You must drink, receive and take in the water He offers in order to be truly satisfied. Too many believers are satisfied with being in a good service and living their life drinking from the wells of others. They are satisfied with just enough of God's presence to get them into heaven. Drinking water from everyone else's well and being in a good service will not satisfy the deep longing of your spirit for God. You must come and *drink* in of the presence of God to be satisfied within.

When we gather together for worship, that is why we are there—to drink living water.

> For by one Spirit we were all baptized into one body—whether Jews or Greeks, whether slaves or free—and have all been made to drink into one Spirit.
>
> —1 CORINTHIANS 12:13

Are you thirsty yet? If not, you will be.

## A Thirsty Woman at the Well

The story of my life has paralleled the story of John 4. The Lord began to touch my heart with the incredible message of this chapter in 1986. Sixteen

years have passed, and it speaks to me today just as
it did back then. Every time I need a little encouragement, I read again this wonderful truth about
how Jesus changed a woman's life by teaching her
how to worship. I shared part of my journey into
worship in my book *Changed in His Presence*, but
God has revealed so many more things to me since
then that I feel compelled to share the truths of
John 4 with you again.

> You must drink, receive
> and take in the water
> He offers in order to be
> truly satisfied.

As I sit here preparing to put these revelations
down on paper, I feel the presence of Lord. With the
help of the Holy Spirit, I believe the Lord wants me
to walk with you through this life-changing chapter
in John. Let me take you on a journey through this
woman's encounter with Jesus, and let's just see
what the Holy Spirit does.

Let's pray as we begin:

> *Wonderful Holy Spirit, You are the great teacher*
> *of the church. Holy Spirit, open our hearts and*
> *give us a greater hunger for You than we have ever*
> *experienced. Let us become encircled by Your pres-*
> *ence here with us. Touch our lives with Your pres-*
> *ence. Open our eyes to the truth of God's Word in*
> *our hearts. Open our ears to hear Your still, small*
> *voice clearly. Open our hearts to receive from Your*
> *wonderful Holy Spirit that our lives may be*
> *changed forever. Make Jesus real, and change us*
> *more and more into His image for the glory of*
> *God. In Jesus' name, amen.*

In John 4, Jesus established a relationship with the Samaritan woman so that we might understand that what He did for her, He will do for us.

God approaches each person as a unique individual worthy of His time and attention.

> The Lord GOD has given Me
> The tongue of the learned,
> That I should know how to speak
> A word in season to him who is weary.
> He awakens Me morning by morning,
> He awakens My ear
> To hear as the learned.
>
> —ISAIAH 50:4

Why is this verse important? Take note that this verse in Isaiah tells us how God values each individual. He will "speak a word in season" to one person, just when that person needs to hear from God the most. That is exactly what He did in John 4. He brought one immoral woman face to face with Himself, revealing to her that her life was headed in the wrong direction.

Does His manner of relating to her sound familiar to you? It does to me. Where would we be without those moments when Jesus meets with us—one by one—and "speaks a word in season"? God had a word in season for a woman who was weary. This is why Jesus said:

> Are you tired? Worn out? Burned out on religion? Come to me. Get away with me and you'll recover your life. I'll show you how to take a real rest.
>
> —MATTHEW 11:28, THE MESSAGE

On that important day recorded in John 4, Jesus had departed from Judea on His way to Galilee. Avoiding the bypass road around Samaria, Jesus instead purposed to travel through Samaria. Scripture says, "But He *needed* to go through Samaria" (John 4:4, emphasis added). On the way to Galilee, the Father intended to minister to this one woman. This woman was thirsty; she was an outcast and full of hurts. She came at midday to this well outside the city walls, expecting no one to be there. She thought this would be just another day at the well trying to satisfy her thirst. But Someone was waiting for her. This day was going to be different from all those other days, because her thirst was about to change. No longer would she try to satisfy her deepest thirst with physical water. That day her deepest thirst—a thirst for a love that would last forever—would be satisfied with living water. God had a word in season for her.

> God approaches each person as a unique individual worthy of His time and attention.

## What's Up With Samaria?

To the religious Pharisees, being a Samaritan was equal to being a demonized pagan. At times they even accused Jesus of the same: "Then Jews answered him, 'Aren't we right in saying that you are a Samaritan and demon-possessed?'" (John 8:48,

NIV). In that day Samaritans were also called *pigs*. They were the forgotten, the hurting, the unloved. In other words, they were prime candidates for a loving Savior. Jesus believed they were the very ones in need of what He offered.

Now that we understand the attitude of the religious Jews toward Samaritans, let's closely observe what Jesus did.

> So He [Jesus] came to a city of Samaria which is called Sychar, near the plot of ground that Jacob gave to his son Joseph. Now Jacob's well was there. Jesus therefore, being wearied from His journey, sat thus by the well. It was about the sixth hour.
>
> —JOHN 4:5–6

## The wells of others cannot satisfy.

It is important to note that Jesus is sitting at Jacob's well. It was to Jacob's well that the Samaritan woman walked each day in an effort to satisfy her deep thirst. We can only guess that as she drudged the half mile to the well from the town, she longed to encounter God as Jacob had and to have her deep thirst satisfied by God as He had satisfied Jacob. (See Genesis 32:22–32.) Perhaps she hoped somehow that the water from his well could satisfy her thirst.

But inheriting a well from our spiritual fathers cannot satisfy. We can honor the well, speak well of the well and remember how our fathers blessed us with it, but it will not satisfy our needs. We must dig our own well by experiencing God's presence for ourselves.

As Jesus sits thus by the well, He becomes the lid, the closure to a well that will no longer satisfy. By

His very presence there, He declares prophetically to the woman, "This well, from which you are so accustomed to drawing, will no longer satisfy you." So used to coming to this well, she was about to go home with a fountain of living water deep inside her. She came with a water pot to draw water, but now she was going to go home with a well of living water. Six significant words will tell her story for all time—"The woman then left her waterpot!" (v. 28).

God is your source.

Jesus and the Samaritan woman were at the well by themselves. She came alone. Where were all her friends? She had been married five times and was living with a sixth man. It's a good guess that all those affairs didn't make her real popular with her friends. She's not only a Samaritan, an outcast to the Jews, but she's probably an outcast to her own people.

Have you ever noticed that it's at moments when you are alone that you are most aware of the emptiness within? No one is there to pump you up, to anoint you with oil or to prophesy over you. It is then that you must acknowledge God as your only source.

Never put all your hope in a person, a place or even a good church with a good pastor. There are many wonderful pastors, leaders and great church families. I believe that God's people are hungry for change, real change! But God alone is the source.

Someone preaching a "pump you up" message will not change you. Shouting the preacher down with, "Preach it, brother. Say it like you mean it," will not change you. Good church programs are not wrong. Good preaching is needed. But it all comes

down to you and Him. Without the presence of
Jesus, none of these things will satisfy you. The pastor is not called to pump you up. The worship
leader's responsibility is not to motivate or inspire
you. These ministry gifts can encourage and motivate, but they cannot change. Great messages and
great music are gone as quickly as they came if the
presence of the Lord is not there. God alone can
pump you up when He alone becomes your source.

So, here's our setting: "A woman of Samaria came
to draw water. Jesus said to her, 'Give Me a drink'"
(v. 7).

## Jesus Comes to Us

Empty, thirsty and dry, she comes to the well alone,
and Jesus speaks to her. The first thing about Jesus to
note is that He did not send her away. He came all the
way from Judea to speak to her. He doesn't ignore her;
He is available to her.

Jesus makes Himself available to you in worship.
He has made Himself available to you by sending
the Holy Spirit. He is saying something like this to
you, "I'm at the right hand of the Father. I'm making intercession for you. I've sent you My Holy
Spirit." He's available through His Holy Spirit to
comfort you and walk alongside of you. He is in
you and with you. The Holy Spirit is always there.
When you are drinking from the well that no longer
satisfies, know that He's available. If you have felt
ostracized, isolated and alone, Jesus makes Himself
available to you right now. You may feel exactly as
this woman felt—empty, dry and alone. Jesus wants

to fill your well with His living water. Just give Him your life, and He will fill it.

What have you done this week that makes Him unavailable to you? Nothing! You see, there is nothing you can do to make Him stop loving you. When you were still in sin, He loved you.

> If you have felt ostracized, isolated and alone, Jesus makes Himself available to you right now.

Worship begins with the understanding that, "God so loved…that He gave His only begotten Son" (John 3:16). Worship begins with God's love. As we receive His love, we respond to it. Worship isn't initiated by our effort; worship is a response to God's love. Paul has written:

> But God demonstrates His own love toward us, in that while we were still sinners, Christ died for us. Much more then, having now been justified by His blood, we shall be saved from wrath through Him.
>
> —ROMANS 5:8–9

Jesus loves you. There is nothing you can do to make Him stop loving you. There was nothing this Samaritan woman could do to isolate herself from God because He is always available. As long as you have breath, He's available. Jesus died for you on the cross and shed His blood for your sin, and there's no way that He is going to reject you. He has already paid the price with His own life for you. He is *Jehovah-Shammah*—the God "who is here."

Jesus invites you to ask for living water. In John 4:7, Jesus asks the Samaritan woman for a drink. She responds, "Why are You asking me for a drink?"

Jesus says to her, "If you knew the gift of God, and who it is who says to you, 'Give Me a drink,' you would have asked Him, and He would have given you living water" (v. 10). What did she have to do to get living water? Simply ask!

Jesus did not ask her to become religious before He would change her life. Yet when given an opportunity to accept the living water Jesus has to offer, some people actually say things like, "Well, I'm going to get cleaned up first," or "I'm going to wear a nice suit and go to church this morning." That is not what God is looking for. The Bible says, "The LORD does not see as man sees; for man looks at the outward appearance, but the LORD looks at the heart" (1 Sam. 16:7).

All she has to do is *ask*! All you have to do is ask. What keeps you from asking?

- *Guilt?* "I feel too guilty to ask Him to fill and change me."

- *Hurt?* "I'm hurting too much to ask. I am not sure that He understands what I'm going through."

- *Shame?* "I'm too ashamed of my past."

- *Fear?* "I'm afraid that God will not receive me."

What is it, then, that kept the Samaritan woman from asking? What keeps you from asking? The truth is, it is not guilt, even though you may feel guilty. It is not hurt, though you may have experienced some. It's not shame, though you feel terrible about the things you've done. It's not even fear. It's pride! You may be too proud to ask.

Jesus called her out of her guilt, hurt, shame and fear by putting His finger on the deepest issues of her past. Then He washed her with clean water. Guilt, hurt, shame and fear will keep you trapped in a cell of unworthiness of God's unconditional love. These things cause you to believe the lie that God has forsaken you. But He has not forsaken you. His promise to you is this:

> For He Himself has said, "I will never leave you nor forsake you."
>
> —HEBREWS 13:5

As the woman at Samaria confronted Jesus at Jacob's well, she began a conversation with Him. The first thing Jesus does is minister to her spirit. He doesn't offer her water—He offers "living water."

> Jesus answered and said to her, "If you knew the gift of God, and who it is who says to you, 'Give Me a drink,' you would have asked Him, and He would have given you *living water*."
>
> —JOHN 4:10, EMPHASIS ADDED

The Greek word for *living* (*zao*) means to enjoy real life, to have vital power and to be fresh water. The first thing God will enliven is your spirit man. He wants to touch your spirit man because there is nothing in the flesh that can satisfy the deep needs of your heart. Only the Spirit of God can satisfy.

Just as the well of Jacob could not satisfy the

thirsting of the Samaritan woman's soul, so too the wells of this world bring no satisfaction to our souls. But the touch of the Spirit goes way beyond the physical or emotional parts of your being. He goes deep inside the heart of every matter. Jesus wants to remove those things that clog your well. All these dealings of the heart are preparation so that the well will spring up in you and will never run dry.

How important is the well within you? After you have been healed and walked in divine health, your physical body will still die one day. After you have experienced every emotional high in your soul, those feelings will end. Only your spirit man will live forever, and that's where the well is. This fountain of living water will never ever run dry. Your spirit will worship Him forever.

## Jesus Ministers to the Heart

The woman's perception of Jesus deepened as she spent time with Him. Watch the succession of her greeting.

1. The woman's first greeting is *Sir*: "The woman said to Him, '*Sir*...'" (John 4:11).

2. The woman's second greeting is *prophet*: "Sir, I perceive that You are a *prophet*" (v. 19).

3. The woman's third greeting is *Christ*: "Could this be the *Christ*?" (v. 29).

First Jesus made Himself available to her and

ministered to her spirit. Then He began to deal with the issue of her heart. When the Lord wants to deal with you, He starts from the inside out. True and lasting change always begins on the inside—not on the outside. It doesn't matter what you look like on the outside. You can't clean yourself up enough to look good on the inside.

> The touch of the Spirit goes way beyond the physical or emotional parts of your being. He goes deep inside the heart of every matter.

Jesus tells her, "Woman, you have been coming to this well, but this well will not satisfy you. You have come to the well, but I'm sending you home with the fountain inside of you." Jesus described for the woman the characteristics of the living water that He had for her. In His words we can identify these characteristics.

> But whoever drinks of the water that I shall give him will never thirst. But the water that I shall give him will become in him a fountain of water springing up into everlasting life.
>
> —JOHN 4:14

Let's look closer at these characteristics of the living water. Notice what Jesus says to the woman:

- *"The water that I shall give"*—These are not just the waters of men, ministry or even the waters of revival. The water's greatest characteristic is that it is Jesus' water. It's not labeled "From the fountain of Ponce de Leon," "Drawn from the Crystal Streams" or with some other designer-water label—it's labeled "From the Fountain of Jesus Christ"! So if you are thirsty, stop running after God's servants and come to Jesus, who alone can give you living water.

- *"Will never thirst"*—This living water will satisfy. No longer will you have to run from service to service, conference to conference.

- *"Will become in him"*—No more need to feel some manifestation externally. The manifestation of this water is on the inside of you.

- *"A fountain of water"*—This is an endless source, a consistent fountain inside you.

- *"Springing up"*—This water source will bubble up like a fountain. It's not a stagnant pond, but an ever-living fountain. This fountain knows "no off-season."

- *"Into everlasting life"*—This supply is not momentary; it's not a temporary supply. This water lasts forever. It is eternal and will continue to live in you forever.

Here is the Samaritan woman's problem. She thought that all she needed was water. Day after day she drudged out to this well to get the water she needed to sustain her life that day. If only she had water, all her needs would be supplied. It's the one thing she needed—and she needed it every day. But Jesus was offering her "living water." She has no comprehension of what Jesus is offering her. At best she thought it might save her the trip out to the well every day. So she said to him, "Give me this water, that I may not thirst, nor come here to draw" (v. 15). She could not comprehend that Jesus offered her living water to satisfy not only her physical thirst—but also living water to satisfy her soul thirst.

## Jesus Demands Accountability

Finally she asks for what He was offering. But there are a few matters of accountability that must be dealt with. Before the living water can flow, repentance must clean out the woman's well deep within. "Jesus said to her, 'Go, call your husband, and come here'" (v. 16).

Jesus knew that this question would open up the most sensitive issue of her heart. He loved her enough to confront her with truth, because He said, "I am the way, the truth, and the life" (John 14:6). You shall know the truth, and the knowledge of the truth will set you free. It's not just truth that sets you free, but the knowledge of truth.

The reason this woman was in this condition was because she was not satisfied in her heart. It was only right for Jesus to speak to her about thirst. She was so thirsty for something real. She had turned to sexual promiscuity to fill the hunger in her heart. Like this woman, too many of us are looking for love in all the wrong places—immoral relationships, pornography, drugs, crime and even religion.

No man could meet her deep spiritual needs. Ladies, there is no man on this planet who can satisfy the deep needs of your spirit, Men, please don't be offended with me, but there is no woman who can meet your deep spiritual needs. Jesus, and only Jesus, can satisfy!

Why did the Pharisees and Sadducees hate Jesus? It wasn't because He challenged them with the Law. It wasn't because He healed the sick or because the multitudes followed Him. It wasn't even because of the miracles, signs and wonders. They hated truth, and all that Jesus embodied was true and real. He was the *truth*. Whenever Jesus was with them, truth was there, and they saw themselves for who and what they really were.

The same was true for this Samaritan woman. When she stood before Jesus, she saw herself for who she really was. God does not expose our sins to condemn us. His purpose for exposing them is to cleanse our lives and rid us of our bondage to sin. For that reason, He will confront you with who you really are.

## Jesus knew the truth of her life.

> The woman answered, "I have no husband." Jesus said to her, "You have well said, 'I have no husband,' for you have had five husbands, and the one whom you now have is not your husband; in that you spoke truly."
>
> —JOHN 4:17–18

How did Jesus know about her husband? Jesus is revealing something that we must all understand: "Woman, I know everything about you."

Wow, Jesus knows you! He knows everything about you. And everything about me.

This is why I love Him so much—He knows everything about me. This makes my relationship with Him so much easier. I can't hide anything from Him. He ministers to the deepest issues of your heart because He knows everything about you.

Jesus holds us accountable and responsible for our lives. There are many believers in the church who resemble this woman. No, they haven't married five times, although some have come close! They love God and go to church faithfully, but they live to satisfy the five natural senses. They live for what they see, hear, taste, smell and feel. Do you live your life trying to satisfy these five natural senses? You are trying to satisfy the longing of your spirit with the external.

It is very obvious from the account of John 4 that the Samaritan woman hadn't been able to satisfy the longing of her soul—even with five husbands. She was running from husband to husband. Like her, there are some in the church who run from church to church like fish jumping fish tanks. They run from one service to another service. They are thinking, *Who's the new pastor on the block? Oh, they have good worship over there. This church has gold falling. Over there they have people falling out in their services.*

Stop running from husband to husband... church to church...thing to thing—and run to Jesus. He is the only one who can feed your inner man, the real you!

I have a word at this point for those in ministry or are aspiring to be in ministry. Remember that your calling to be an apostle, prophet, evangelist, pastor or teacher can never satisfy. "And He Himself gave some to be apostles, some prophets, some evangelists, and some pastors and teachers" (Eph. 4:11).

At times, men and women marry the ministry instead of falling in love with the Bridegroom. For years I have heard great teachings about remaining pure in ministry. "The three keys to keeping your ministry pure," I have heard, "are: Don't touch the glory. Don't touch the gold. Don't touch women." These three keys are very important, and most ministers would never be guilty of these things. However, many are living for their gifts, their positions, their titles, doctrines or denominations.

Being in the ministry will never satisfy the deep needs of your spirit. Holding an important ministerial position or possessing a supernatural gifting will not satisfy your deepest longings. Only Jesus can satisfy! We may preach great messages about how to be set free from addictions and bondages to drugs and alcohol, and all the while be addicted ourselves to the office of the ministry. Don't let it happen to you.

When we finally find the lover of our soul, like the woman in the Song of Solomon, we sing:

> When I found the one I love.
> I held him and would not let him go…
> —SONG OF SOLOMON 3:4

The woman at the well in Samaria had been married to five men and was shacking up with the sixth. But once she encountered Jesus at the well of Samaria and tasted the living water He offered to her, she recognized that it wasn't another man she needed to satisfy her soul. She "left her waterpot, went her way into the city, and said to the men... 'Could this be the Christ?'" (John 4:28–29). She met Christ Himself, and He sent her home with a fountain of living water bubbling up and flowing out of her. No longer did she have to draw water that could not quench her thirst from a well that never satisfied. She carried the fountain of living water deep within her soul. Now she had become the well.

> Being in the ministry will never satisfy the deep needs of your spirit.

We read the results in verse 39: "Many of the Samaritans of that city believed in Him because of the word of the woman."

When you encounter the Christ at the point of your greatest need and drink of His living water until you become a fountain bubbling up and flowing forth, you will never thirst again. Now you are the well!

## Worship Is Not Where, but Who

Notice that it was the woman who first mentioned worship, not Jesus:

> The woman said to Him... "Our fathers worshiped on this mountain, and you Jews say that in Jerusalem is the place where one ought to worship." Jesus said to her, "Woman, believe Me, the hour is coming when you will neither on this mountain, nor in Jerusalem, worship the Father. You worship what you do

not know; we know what we worship, for salvation is of the Jews."

—JOHN 4:19–22

Try to imagine this encounter. Here is a despised, sinful Samaritan woman debating worship with the Son of God! Trying desperately to define what she understood to be worship, she brought up the old argument that worship was associated with where you worship. Immediately Jesus corrects her misunderstanding. He teaches here that the important thing is not where you worship; it is whom you worship. Worship is no longer to be associated with a mountain, a place, a city or a time. Now you will worship the Father.

People have asked me, "Where do you worship?" Worship is not a place or even a time. Even in Spirit-filled churches, worship is still associated with a time. "If you want to worship the right way, you begin worship at 10:00 A.M.!"

Others ask, "Where do you go to church?" Often we say to one another, "Come on; we're going to church this morning." Recognize this: You have never gone to church; you ARE the church! We are the temple or the tabernacle of the Holy Spirit.

Look at Jesus' heart. He says to her, "Woman, believe Me." This is His heart for you today. He knows everything about you. He knows every husband—every unproductive, unloving relationship you have had trying to find love in all the wrong places. Now Jesus is holding you accountable for knowing the truth. It's time to focus your worship on whom you worship, not on where you worship.

## Kissing the Face of God

Jesus concluded, "But the hour is coming, and now is, when the true worshipers will worship the Father in spirit and truth; for the Father is seeking such to worship Him" (v. 23). Why would Jesus say her, "when *true* worshipers..."? I believe Jesus was giving a clear distinction that some are *false* worshipers. The church is full of worshipers, but how many really touch Him? He is after those who not only love Him, but who are *in love* with Him, those who are not ashamed to respond to His love with worship. They shall worship the Father and know Him personally, not as God, but as Father.

The way to worship God is to worship Him in spirit and truth. Jesus tells us this in back-to-back verses, so it must be very important. Why? Because nothing draws you closer into His presence than true worship.

> God is Spirit, and those who worship Him
> must worship in spirit and truth.
>
> —JOHN 4:24

True worship is not easy to define, but I know this: The only thing that will fulfill and satisfy the longing of your heart is worshiping the Father in spirit and truth.

In the Old Testament the Hebrew word for *worship*, *shachah*, means "to depress, to lie prostrate in homage to royalty or God." In worship one bows down or falls down flat as one stretches out with face to the ground.

In the New Testament the word for *worship* is the

Greek word *proskuneo*, which means "to kiss, like a dog licking his master's hand." The Greek concept is to bow before one's feet and to lean forward in a token of reverence. The Old Testament worship bows in reverence. The New Testament worship adds a kiss.

God created creatures that do nothing else but bow in worship. He desires something more from us as His new creation (2 Cor. 5:17). He wants intimacy! Intimacy with Jesus, intimacy with the Holy Spirit and intimacy with the Father. Bowing is important and has its place in worship. True worship eliminates the distance between God and the worshiper. God desires to be kissed. In Psalm 2:12, we read, "Kiss the Son, lest He be angry."

I woke up early on a recent morning with this thought just pounding on my heart: *Some will kiss Him and betray Him, while others will kiss Him and worship Him.* Not every kiss is a kiss of worship. Judas greeted Jesus with a kiss—but it was a kiss of betrayal. Please let every kiss of yours be a kiss of worship and not a kiss of betrayal!

## True worship eliminates the distance between God and the worshiper.

The Samaritan woman now begins to realize to whom she is talking. Her curiosity rises, and she says, "I know that Messiah is coming...When He comes, He will tell us all things" (John 4:25). She's asking, "Could You be the one?"

Jesus responded, "I who speak to you am He" (v. 26). In the original Greek, this verse is so powerful.

It actually says, "The One who stands before you, God, the I AM, I AM is here."

She has met the Son face to face—and she is changed. She runs into the village and tells everyone about Jesus. She has worshiped. She has kissed the face of God.

That's the kind of worship God is seeking. We are worship. With our lives of worship we too can kiss the face of God. In holy intimacy the veil that once covered our faces has been removed. Now the worshiper comes face to face with God and is transformed into His likeness.

> And we, who with unveiled faces all reflect the Lord's glory, are being transformed into his likeness with ever-increasing glory, which comes from the Lord, who is the Spirit.
> —2 CORINTHIANS 3:18, NIV

Are you longing for Jesus? Are you ready to come face to face with God? Are you ready to kiss the face of God with your life of worship?

You may be asking, "What must I do to become a true worshiper? How do I kiss the face of God?" This might sound way too simple, but nonetheless it is truth. Just fall in love with Christ all over again. Tell Him how much you love Him and need Him. He is the only one who will satisfy the longing of your heart.

Only in His presence can you be changed again and again. The more you fall in love with Jesus, the more Jesus changes you from glory to glory. This is what worship is all about. Just tell Him, "Lord Jesus, I love You more than ever before. How I love You,

Jesus! You mean so much to me. Lord, I love You more than the church, more than ministry."

I pray that the Lord will touch your heart with His presence. Renew your love and relationship with Him. Come back to the source of all living water and drink of Him. Leave your old waterpot. Let Him shape you into a new waterpot. There is a well of living water inside of you. Spring up, O well, spring up!

Now, put your hand on your mouth, look up and blow Him a big kiss. Say passionately, "Jesus, I love You."

# To Kiss God's Face...

1. Be born of water and the Spirit.

2. Repent and let His living water clean out your well.

3. Drink from no other well except His well of living water.

4. Let rivers of living water flow out of you.

5. Don't focus on where you worship; fix your eyes on whom you worship—Jesus.

6. Prepare for change. True worship involves God changing you from the inside out.

7. When you find the One you love, never let Him go!

# Chapter 5

## *Talking* Face *to* Face

As I reflect on some of the most memorable times in my life, I realize that, almost without fail, these were times when I came to a crossroad in my walk with the Lord. Times of great hunger in my life were met with great changes, moments when the Lord's presence became more and more real.

Every memorable life experience carries with it a greater revelation of God. I am reminded now of one of those times when I was so hungry for more of Him. I believe that the reason the Lord reminded me of this moment is so that I may encourage and help you in your walk with Jesus.

Several years ago my wife, Erika, and I went away on a much-needed vacation. God has blessed me with such wonderful gifts in my wife and kids. This was one of those times when Erika and I needed to get away and be together.

On the second night of our vacation, the Lord woke me up at four in the morning and said, "Sam, today I want to spend thirty minutes with you."

I sat up and looked at the clock and said, "Lord, I will give You a half-hour today." I lay back down. Just as my head hit the pillow, God said, "Now!"

I got up, took my Bible and went out the balcony. I always begin my time in prayer by reading one of the psalms, so I opened my Bible to pray out of Psalm 119 and Psalm 51. When I finished reading, I closed my Bible and began to worship the Lord. Something was very different. I felt no presence of the Lord.

Remember this: When you do not feel the presence of the Lord, He hasn't moved; you have. God is omnipresent. He is always with us. God never forsakes us. Certainly our feelings are real, but they're not reality. God is always present to us; we are not always present to Him. There was something in me keeping God at a distance.

I knew something was hindering our relationship, so I simply continued to pray. When you feel distant from God, don't give up. Be persistent in your prayer. Press in and pray for as long as it takes to move from superficiality to intimacy with God. Finally, I heard these words, "Be quiet. Be silent."

## When you do not feel the presence of the Lord, He hasn't moved; you have.

This was something I had not heard God express to me before. I honestly did not know how to be quiet in prayer. I learned a profound lesson that morning. First, I learned that my life of expressive worship alone was not enough to get me into His presence. The longer I was quiet, the more real His presence became.

Something was different and more intimate about this time with the Lord. I cried for the next hour and a half. This was so unusual. I had not experienced such a pure and beautiful presence of Jesus. My tears finally stopped, and so did my words. I returned to the motel room about 6:30 A.M. and could not believe those two hours had gone by with very few words spoken. A few hours later my wife and I went down to the beach. I knew that the Lord was not done with me and that there was more to come, so I took my Bible with me. We got settled, and I opened my Bible to Revelation 8 and began to read these words:

> When He opened the seventh seal, there was silence in heaven for about half an hour.
>
> —Revelation 8:1

I realized that God was confirming what had just begun in my life during that half-hour I spent alone with Him. The next morning about 3:00 A.M., the Lord spoke again, saying, "I want to spend thirty minutes alone with you today."

As I got up and went outside, I discovered it was different this morning—His presence was waiting for me. I sat very quietly in the most beautiful atmosphere of God's presence. I was beginning to learn that silence could become an important door for entering into God's presence.

Then the Holy Spirit began to speak to me, "Sam, all I hear from you is about your needs, weakness and longings. All I hear in your prayer are your problems and what you're going through. Sam, do you want to know what the secret is? Learn to be quiet and still. Wait until I come as I have the last two nights. When I come and fill you, then pray, and I will hear and answer you."

What a lesson I learned that day about *being still and knowing God.*

The next day Erika and I were getting ready to go out to lunch. While I was waiting for my wife, I opened the nightstand drawer at our hotel. I saw a book about the hotel owner and his life story. I knew I didn't have much time, so I quickly scanned through the first few pages. The third page hit me like a ton of bricks.

On that page the author was sharing about his mother, who was a praying woman. His mother had instilled in him the fact that when he came face to face with trials and adversities, he should immediately stop what he was doing and spend thirty minutes alone with God. This was the second confirmation the Lord had given me about my time with Him, and my prayer life in the following days changed drastically. From that time on, over the next few years the Lord would wake me up, morning after morning, just to fellowship quietly with Him.

Now, several years later, I know why the Lord has reminded me of that time. Today I really want Him more than I wanted Him back then. I really miss my time with Him. I desperately need to get reacquainted with the secret place we shared in those quiet times together.

How about you?

- Do you miss the secret place, the quiet place of His presence?

- Do you spend way too much time talking and not enough time listening?

- How is your fellowship with the Holy Spirit?

- Are you too busy just to sit and quietly wait for Him without words?

I want to remind you just how much God loves you today. God wants to manifest Himself to you. The same God who showed Himself to Moses wants to reveal Himself to you.

Where do you start? You start by being faithful to God by spending time with Him. Wait quietly for Him; be still and weigh your words before Him. Don't start your day by telling Him about all your needs and problems. He already knows all that you have need of. This may not be an easy thing for you to do. You may find it difficult to sit still and be silent. But it will be worth your effort.

## Be Still and Know

Listen to what God is saying to you and me:

> Be still, and know that I am God;
> I will be exalted among the nations,
> I will be exalted in the earth!
>
> —PSALM 46:10

In the Hebrew language, the words "Be still" give the impression, "to come to nothing." Leave matters with God. Let Him deal with the issues in your

life. Your efforts are not needed. Just relax, and He
will take care of things for you. Exodus 14:13 paints
this picture beautifully: "Stand still, and see the salvation of the LORD." Many victories have been
aborted because we have not learned to be still. We
worry about everything. Stop worrying. Don't panic.
Get rid of the anxiety, and trust God. He will bring
you through, just as He promised.

Do you remember the story of Elijah and the
prophets of Baal in 1 Kings 18? Those pagan
prophets and Elijah, prophet of the one true God,
duel it out on Mount Carmel. The false prophets cry
out all day for Baal to consume their sacrifice with
fire, thereby demonstrating that Baal is real. Of
course nothing happens. Then Elijah, who has
soaked and surrounded his sacrifice with water, prays
to the living God, and fire rains down from heaven.
Baal and its prophets are destroyed. The living God
and His prophet, Elijah, have won a great victory.

However, Queen Jezebel had promoted Baal worship in Israel. Angrily, she ordered her soldiers to
kill Elijah. Fleeing for his life, Elijah ran into the
wilderness and climbed Mount Horeb, the mountain of God. There Elijah hid in a cave and
bemoaned his fate.

Now it's time to face God. 1 Kings 19:11–12
records:

> Then He said, "Go out, and stand on the
> mountain before the LORD." And behold, the
> LORD passed by, and a great and strong wind
> tore into the mountains and broke the rocks
> in pieces before the LORD, but the LORD was
> not in the wind; and after the wind an

> earthquake, but the LORD was not in the
> earthquake; and after the earthquake a fire,
> but the LORD was not in the fire; and after the
> fire a still small voice.

We would expect that a great manifestation of the
Lord would shake Elijah back into reality. We would
expect that God would manifest His presence and
power through mighty acts like whirlwinds, earth-
quakes and fire. But God was in none of those manifestations. The presence of the Lord came to Elijah
in the stillness. God spoke through the silence with
"the sound of gentle whispering."

Only when every other voice is stilled will we
hear God's voice. Only when the voices without and
within us are silenced will we be able to discern the
gentle whisper of God in the stillness. Are you willing to silence every other voice to hear Him?

## Praying in the Stillness

One Thursday night, I was putting my little girl to
bed for the night. While I was praying for her, the
Lord touched my heart and showed me something
about His love for me. In that simple prayer for my
daughter, the Lord revealed His love for me that
night. Shortly thereafter I was getting ready for my
bedtime, and I began to thank the Lord for showing
His love to me.

While I was thanking Him, the Holy Spirit whispered a question, "How did you get to know your
little girl?"

"Lord," I said, "I got to know her by spending
time with her and by talking to her."

His response was, "That's how you get to know Me. You do it by spending time with Me and by talking with Me."

There is a time to be silent and a time to speak. There is such a hunger in the heart of people for prayer. But people are not only struggling in prayer—they are even struggling to find the time to pray. Prayer has become a big bore. How can it be that in the midst of this kind of hunger, prayer is such a burden? When the Holy Spirit is missing, then prayer becomes such a burden to carry.

My little girl has helped me to learn a very valuable lesson about prayer. You see, Christa will not go to sleep until *Daddy* prays for her. When I am away ministering, she will call and remind me, "Daddy, pray for me."

Prayer is her priority before bedtime. Every night as I pray for her, the Lord reminds me about my prayer priority. Prayer is talking to God and getting to know Him. If you desire to know Him, just as in any other relationship, you must spend time talking with Him.

Don't become familiar with what the devil has to say and unfamiliar with what God has to say.

Let's come back to what is truly a priority in our lives. Whose face do you seek first in the morning? How do you spend the first few minutes of your day? Do you give the first minutes of the day to reading the newspaper, getting caught up on world news or watching CNN? Watching the news will not build your faith, but reading His Word will.

Don't become familiar with what the devil has to say and unfamiliar with what God has to say. The enemy loves to mess with your mind by distracting you with worldly things. I am not saying that we should not pay attention to world events in the news. But the call to prayer should not be based on what you saw on TV. When you give the first minutes of your day to these things, the enemy will mess with your head, and prayer then becomes a burden.

## Talking Face to Face With God

My voice You shall hear in the morning, O
   LORD;
In the morning I will direct it to You,
And I will look up.

—PSALM 5:3

"My voice You will hear in the morning." In the morning you set your spirit for the day. We should start our mornings with God, not with television or a newspaper. A cup of coffee and reading the newspaper will not answer prayer. The morning, afternoon and evening will be so much better when we start the day with God. When God is first in our thoughts in the morning, then He will be our last thought at the end of the day.

In the same verse David said, "In the morning I will direct it to You." "God, I am going to direct my prayer to You. You are my focus." Remember that Jesus told the Samaritan woman that worship must be directed to the Father. Prayer and worship are both directed to the Father.

"And I will look up." Prayer will always take you to a higher level in your relationship with God. Prayer will lift you out of your earthly situations and give you God's perspective. Moses had that kind of experience.

One day the Lord said to His friend Moses, "Come up in the morning to Mount Sinai, and present yourself there to Me on the top of the mountain" (Exod. 34:2). There was a purpose to this invitation—God knew that Moses would never understand the children of Israel just by living among them. When he went up the mountain in the morning and looked down from God's view, things were very different. Things will look very different when you are at the top of a mountain. Your view is higher and clearer. Then Moses marched back down the mountain with God's commandments.

In the same way that we do not initiate worship, we also do not initiate prayer. Prayer is God's invitation to us, and we simply respond to it. We see this in the garden with Adam and Eve in Genesis 3. Adam and Eve first heard the voice of God, then they responded to it. God was calling them; they were not calling God.

How did they respond to His voice? They heard it and hid themselves. Today it doesn't seem much different than in the garden. He calls, and no one answers. He calls, and we are hiding in our jobs, in our homes and, yes, even at church.

Prayer is your fellowship with God. God placed in the heart of every believer the desire to pray. This desire originates in God, then comes down to earth and returns back to God in prayer. When you were born again, the desire to pray was put inside of you. Prayer is what alerts you, in the same way that an alarm clock wakes you up. Prayer is what awakens your heart to His desires. The purpose of prayer is to bring you out of the flesh and into the presence of God.

> ## God wants to transform your desire for prayer into a life of prayer.

Prayer, just like worship, can have many hindrances. It's hard to believe that with all the books written about prayer, so few people actually pray. We have heard and read much revelation *about* prayer, but we still have a hard time being faithful *to do it*.

## What Causes Prayerlessness?

I have spent countless hours talking with people who are struggling with prayer. These are not weird or strange folks. Some of them I have known for many years, and outwardly everything looks great. It seems to me that over the years there have been two major things that rob them of time with God.

1. *Self-satisfaction.* That is to say, things were going so well for them that they didn't need God. Their prayer life consisted of praying when things got bad and they needed something from God. When things were going well, they had nothing to pray about.

2. *Distractions.* They were so busy with *doing*

and not *being*. They began to live for
their distractions. Distractions are those
things in your life that keep you in
bondage to that which is not important.

Life presents itself with so many important things
that must be done. The truth is that when this life is
over, you take nothing with you except what you
have done for the cause of eternity. What you have
sown to build His kingdom and how many you
bring with you to heaven are all that count eternally.

God wants to transform your desire for prayer
into a life of prayer. Paul writes, "Devote yourselves
to prayer, being watchful and thankful" (Col. 4:2,
NIV). One of the things that I struggled with for
many years was not having a disciplined prayer life.
Every time I got so busy doing ministry, I had to
remind myself, "It's not about ministry." My prayer
life changed when I was no longer focused on getting God's answers, but on getting God.

## Kissing the Face of God in Prayer

Paul writes, "And because you are sons, God has sent
forth the Spirit of His Son into your hearts, crying out,
'Abba, Father!'" (Gal. 4:6). In prayer we often tend to
focus on the things we need, but the most important
thing in prayer is our relationship with God. Prayer is
birthed out of relationship between the Father and
His sons and daughters. The Lord has blessed me with
four children. When my kids need me, all they have to
say is "Dad," and my ears perk right up. I respond to
their need immediately.

Because we are sons and daughters, we cry out,

"Abba, Father!" Jesus taught His disciples not just *how* to pray. He taught them to pray *and say*, "Our Father." What moves the heart of God is not what you say in prayer. He is moved by the fact that you have come to seek Him in prayer. Hallelujah!

In Genesis 18 we read about a man named Abraham, a man who was not just a hero in the faith but a man who stood still before the Lord. In verse 17 we read, "And the LORD said, 'Shall I hide from Abraham what I am doing…?'"

Psalm 25:14 says, "The secret of the LORD is with those who fear Him, and He will show them His covenant." When God makes a covenant with you, He will not hide His plan from you.

God intended to destroy Sodom and Gomorrah, but He didn't want to hide it from Abraham. God makes this incredible statement: "For I have known him, in order that he may command his children and his household after him, that they keep the way of the LORD…" (Gen. 18:19). God's judgment arose because of how great the sin was in these cities. He said, "I will go down now and see what they have done" (v. 21).

But this is what God discovered:

> Then the men turned away from there and went toward Sodom, *but Abraham still stood before the LORD.*
> —GENESIS 18:22, EMPHASIS ADDED

Everybody else took off, but Abraham got in the face of God. While all the others walked away, Abraham stood still before the Lord. Please read the rest of this chapter. It really is incredible. I will only give you the short version.

Abraham began to plead with God. I would paraphrase what he said this way, "God, I know You, and I know why You told me about Your plans for Sodom and Gomorrah. You told me because You really don't want to do what You have to do. Can we talk? Would You also destroy the righteous with the wicked? What if You found fifty righteous people? Would You destroy the place and not spare it for the fifty? No, no; far be it from You to do something like this; shall not the Judge of all the earth do right?"

Then Abraham said, "Look, I know I am but dust and might become ashes, but I need to talk to You." He was on a mission, and he continued to stand before the Lord. "OK, how about forty-five…suppose there were forty?"

God said, "I will not destroy it for the sake of forty."

Then Abraham proceeded to bargain with God all the way down to ten. God agreed to spare the city for ten righteous people. But there were not ten righteous people there.

God had made a covenant earlier with Abraham. Now He was planning to destroy the cities of Sodom and Gomorrah. But because of His relationship in covenant with Abraham, He said, "I can't hide this from Abraham." God told Abraham what He was going to do. As a result, Abraham stood still before the Lord. His prayer life stood still and waited for God to move.

In our nation today, there is a move of God going on right now. God is calling many intercessors to stand in the gap in preparation for the greatest revival we have ever seen. Prayer is a call to intercession to seek the face of God.

> When You said, "Seek My face,"
> My heart said to You, "Your face, LORD, I will
> seek."
> —PSALM 27:8

There is a difference between seeking God and seeking God's face.

- Are you in front of Him?
- Behind Him?
- Are you near Him or before Him?

There is nothing wrong if all you desire is to seek Him, but something happens when you seek His face. When my children want to talk to me, I don't say, "Talk to the hand." They don't talk to my back, my feet or my hands. They talk face to face with Dad.

Do you know how much God desires for you to get in His face? He wants you to get yourself right in the middle of what He is doing. He loves you so much. The next time you pray, don't just seek God—*but seek His face*. Scripture instructs us, "My sons, do not be negligent now [misled, deceived], for the Lord has chosen you to *stand before Him* [*paw-neem*, "to face, as the part that turns"], to serve Him, and that you should minister to Him" (2 Chron. 29:11, emphasis added).

Why is it some people often are in a place of worship, and yet they are not changing? It is because they neglect their prayer closet. God wants us to hunger after His presence. If you want to find God

quickly, then come thirsting for Him. We will find
Him when we have searched for Him with all our
hearts. "He has satisfied the hungry with good
things..." (Luke 1:53, NLT).

# Prayer is a call to intercession to seek the face of God.

God is calling us into a deeper level of prayer and
intercession. Prayer will prepare our hearts for true
worship. Prayer brings honor to God. Prayer is an act
of our worship. Prayer brings us to a place of total
dependency upon God. God is not reluctant to
answer our prayer. In fact, prayer enables us to receive
all His promises. Our goal in prayer and worship
must always be to have communion with God. How
do you learn to worship? By worshiping! How do you
learn to pray? By praying! Let's get back to the closet.

# Kissing the Face of God for Your Family

God wants more than an eternal relationship with
you. He wants all of your family, your household,
saved as well. You may have lost loved ones—a
spouse, children, parents, grandparents and various
relatives. God desires for all to be saved.

In my culture, we often greet one another with a
kiss. At times, we bring a kiss from one family mem-
ber to another. Sometimes I will visit one of my
brothers, and then I will see my mom. As I greet her,
I kiss her, thus bringing my brother's kiss to her. In

kissing her, her memory of her love for him is stirred, and she will often weep.

In Acts 10 we read of how Cornelius prayed and offered alms to God. In doing so, he built a memorial before God. As a result of this, Cornelius and all of his household was saved. I want you to follow Cornelius's example of prayer. Build a memorial before the face of God. Kiss His face often with your prayers. Remind the Lord of how much He loves your lost family members. Ask God to send His Holy Spirit to stir every believer who crosses the path of your lost loved ones so that they will show forth the love of God in everything they say or do in relationship to your lost loved one.

As you pray, cover God's face with memorial kisses as a constant reminder of your desire to see your loved ones saved.

## Be Still…

Take time right this moment. Stop reading. Start praying. Stop making noise with your lips; begin listening with your heart. Be still. Draw near to the living God.

Often when my daughter whispers to me, I must draw close to her face in order to hear the secret she wants to share with me. In God's secret place, you must silence every other noise and voice. Then you must draw close to His face in the stillness in order to hear His whisper.

As you listen to God's whisper, your ear will be close to His lips.

Your heart will be knit to His.
And in that moment time will stand still.
Eternity will invade your soul,
and you will kiss the face of God.

## To Kiss God's Face...

1. Draw apart from the noises and distractions around you. Be still and pray.

2. Listen for God's gentle whisper.

3. Make prayer your first priority in the morning.

4. Intercede for others.

5. Desire God more than answers.

6. Pray for your lost family members.

7. Build a memorial of prayer with your kisses.

# Chapter 6

## *Show* Me *Your* Glory

**M**any people are talking about the glory of God today. It's like Surround Sound in the body of Christ. People are hungrier for more of God than ever before. People cry out desperately for God's glory. God's people have heard all the messages, sung all the songs and even experienced His power through miracles; yet, they are left knowing there must be more. They hear something off in the distance.

There is a strong impression in my spirit of the sound of an abundance of rain. When a rainstorm is off in the distance, you can see it coming because the clouds thicken and become darker. The rain begins with a few drops at first, but before long it becomes a blinding sheet of water.

We are seeing the first few drops of a coming downpour of God's glory. Its beginning is like a sun shower, but as the hunger grows in God's people, the gentle rain will become a rising tide. Glory will cover our ankles, enabling us to walk in it. It will surround our knees as we pray in it. It will encircle our waists as intercession, and then it will become a rising tide for the End-Time harvest.

As I write this, Central Florida has been experiencing drought and is in critical need of rain. Our church has been praying for both natural rain and for the rain of His presence. A few days ago we had a rainstorm. After the first few drops, my two younger children announced, "We're going outside to play in the rain."

Adults are so different. At the first sign of rain we look for cover. We scramble for umbrellas, hats, newspapers—anything to keep the rain off our heads. I watched my children play in the rain from inside at a window. They were having a blast, and they motioned repeatedly for me to join them. (I don't think so!) As the wind picked up and the clouds grew darker, it soon became a heavy downpour, and they ran back into the house.

> The purpose of God's glory is to change our garments. He wants to give you a new garment of His presence to wear.

The Spirit of God began to speak to my heart about the glory of God. The glory of God, like the rain, is picking up in intensity. We have been having fun with the first few sprinkles, enjoying the manifestations. But as the rain intensifies, so does our responsibility. God's glory must produce CHANGE!

The coming rain of God will not be in the realm of

manifestations; it will be a realm of glory. This wave of His presence will bring the End-Time revival and harvest—revival for inside the church and the harvest for outside the church. We cannot remain ignorant about the purpose of His glory and presence. The purpose for the glory of God is not to produce gold flakes, manna, laughter, feathers or falling out. These are merely manifestations. The purpose of God's glory is to change our garments. He wants to give you a new garment of His presence to wear.

## What Is the Glory of God?

The glory of God cannot be fully understood by being taught. It must be experienced! Like the old adage says, "It's better felt than telt!" But once you have tasted His glory, you will not want to go back.

Let's look at what God's Word says about His glory. To understand the glory of God, we really have to go back to the garden. In the Garden of Eden, God gave Adam and Eve His presence and fellowship. Adam was *clothed* with the glory of God.

Originally, humanity was crowned or clothed in God's glory.

> What is man that You are mindful of him,
> And the son of man that you visit him?
> For You have made him a little lower than the
> angels,
> And You have crowned [clothed] him with
> glory and honor.
> —PSALM 8:4–5

Glory is defined as the outer garment of the iridescence of God, the splendor rays of God. This garment of light is what clothed Adam and Eve in the garden. Adam was created to live in the presence of God, but when Adam sinned, his innocence of being was lost. God never cut Adam off from His presence—it was Adam who hid. Adam was still in God's presence, but he was no longer clothed in God's glory because of sin.

For the first time, Adam realized he was naked. In his shame, he hid from God's presence. Now I have a question for you. If God were to manifest His presence to you, would you be looking for a place to hide?

> Then the eyes of both of them were opened, and they knew that they were naked; and they sewed fig leaves together and made themselves coverings. And they heard the sound of the LORD God walking in the garden in the cool of the day, and Adam and his wife hid themselves from the presence of the LORD God among the trees of the garden.
>
> —GENESIS 3:7–8

No one can tell us how long Adam was in the garden. In Eden man lived in an eternal realm until man sinned. In this timeless realm there was no need for miracles; there was no sickness there. Adam lived in a continual revelation of God; he lived in a sinless environment. Time as we know it did not begin until man sinned. God said to man, "In the day that you eat…you shall surely die" (Gen. 2:17).

God's Word tells us Adam lived to be nine hundred thirty years old. When man fell, he began to conform to time instead of eternity. It took Adam more than nine hundred years to catch up to his own death. My prayer today is, "God, bring us into the realm of Your glory that Adam once knew!"

The glory speaks of God's standard for holiness and moral integrity. Paul writes, "For all have sinned and fall short of the glory of God" (Rom. 3:23). What does it mean to fall short? It means "to lack or to be without" the glory of God. The glory of God is the radiance, the splendor, the outward manifestation of what He is.

The glory of God also speaks of the brightness of God. Jesus never sinned, which is why He is called "the brightness of His glory." We read this in Hebrews 1:3: "...who [Jesus] being the brightness of His glory and the express image of His person, and upholding all things by the word of His power, when He had by Himself purged our sins, sat down at the right hand of the Majesty on high."

As the second Adam, Jesus enters as the eternal Word into time and space. How is He clothed? With God's garment of glory, of course. "And the Word became flesh and dwelt among us, and we beheld His glory, the glory as of the only begotten of the Father, full of grace and truth" (John 1:14).

For a fleeting moment, the disciples glimpsed Jesus' garment of glory on the Mount of Transfiguration. "He [Jesus] was transfigured before them. His face shone like the sun, and His clothes became as white as the light" (Matt. 17:2-3).

Remember that sin and shame strip off the garment of glory, leaving us naked and ashamed (Gen. 3:8-9). On the cross, Jesus bore our sin and shame, being crucified naked. In the moment He took upon Himself our transgression, that garment of glory clothing Him from His human conception, and seen by the disciples on the Mount of Transfiguration, was exchanged for a garment of sin and shame. The agony of that exchange caused Jesus to cry out, "My God, my God, why hast thou forsaken me?" (Matt. 27:46, KJV).

Clothed in His glory, you become a "glory cloud" for others to witness and see the power of Jesus Christ living in us.

But God raised Jesus from the dead and clothed Him once again and forever with glory: "...God, who raised Him [Jesus] from the dead and gave Him glory" (1 Pet. 1:21). When you and I receive Christ as Lord of our lives, we too are clothed with His glory and reflect His likeness:

> Therefore we were buried with Him through baptism into death, that just as Christ was raised from the dead by the glory of the Father, even so we also should walk in newness of life. For if we have been united together in the likeness of His death, certainly we also shall be in the likeness of His resurrection.
>
> —ROMANS 6:4–5

Within every believer is deposited through Christ's resurrection power "the hope of glory" (Col. 1:27).

The apostle John writes in a similar way: "Beloved,

now we are children of God; and it has not yet been revealed what we shall be, but we know that when He is revealed, we shall be like Him, for we shall see Him as He is. And everyone who has this hope in Him purifies himself, just as He is pure" (1 John 3:2–3). What is the hope? It is the hope of glory. This fulfills the prayer of Jesus in John 17:22, "And the glory which You gave Me I have given them, that they may be one just as We are one." You and I have been clothed with His glory.

## The Shekinah Glory of God

Better known as the "glory cloud," this light lit up the holy of holies in the tabernacle. It was the light source. During the forty years of Israel's journey through the wilderness, the cloud of glory hovered over the tabernacle, and the whole multitude of Israel could see its glow all night long.

> Then the cloud covered the tabernacle of meeting, and the glory of the LORD filled the tabernacle. And Moses was not able to enter the tabernacle of meeting, because the cloud rested above it, and the glory of the LORD filled the tabernacle. Whenever the cloud was taken up from above the tabernacle, the children of Israel would go onward in all their journeys. But if the cloud was not taken up, then they did not journey till the day that it was taken up. For the cloud of the LORD was above the tabernacle by day, and fire was over it by night, in the sight of all the house of Israel, throughout all their journeys.
>
> —EXODUS 40:34–38

Clothed in His glory, you become a "glory cloud" for others to witness and see the power of Jesus Christ living in us. So many people seem to be longing for some mystical manifestation of a haze filling a sanctuary and producing some sort of glory droplets on the people or the furnishings. What really happens is that His likeness, His glory is so reflected in our lives that the lost are saved, the sick are healed and the bound are delivered. Now that's truly a manifestation of God's glory in Christ Jesus!

## The Glory of God in the Life of Moses

There are many valuable lessons in Moses' life about the glory of God. This man hungered after God more than any other in the Old Testament. He hungered after God very early in life. His first lesson about God's glory came at the burning bush. "Then He said, 'Do not draw near this place. Take your sandals off your feet, for the place where you stand is holy ground'" (Exod. 3:5).

Moses' relationship with God began with an introduction to God's holiness. When he removed his sandals and his feet hit that ground, the burning that began at his feet burned into his heart with the holiness of God. God's glory is always preceded by His holiness. When you cry out for God's glory, be prepared. He will require a new level of holiness in your life.

Moses also learned to stay in the presence of God. He desired God, not the miracles. Moses would not

settle for anything less than God Himself. Moses
loved the presence of God and stayed in it.

> The LORD said to Moses, "Come up to me on
> the mountain and stay here, and I will give you
> the tablets of stone, with the law and com-
> mands I have written for their instruction."
> —EXODUS 24:12, NIV

God doesn't want just to touch you with His presence; He wants you to stay with Him. Way too many
people in the church are living from service to service, one momentary touch to another.

Moses wanted to know Him! Can you see that
this must be the primary purpose for why we desire
Him? It must always be about knowing Him. The
reason so many people do not live in the presence
of God is because they want Him for all the wrong
reasons. To know Him means that we must become
intimate with Him, not just know *about* Him, but
know *Him*.

> ## God doesn't want just to touch you with His presence; He wants you to stay with Him.

Moses pleaded, "Now therefore, I pray, if I have
found grace in Your sight, show me now Your way,
that I may know You and that I may find grace in Your
sight" (Exod. 33:13). Moses had a pure desire…a
pure motive…a pure prayer for desiring more of God.
He wasn't after a ministry, a title or his own show. I
can almost imagine him crying out so deeply, "God, I
want You. I want Your presence because I want to

know You." Our motive in seeking power must be pure, honest and for God's glory alone, because God will not share His glory. When we ask God for His glory, our motive must be pure.

The Lord's response to Moses is so very powerful:

> And He said, "My Presence will go with you, and I will give you rest." Then he said to Him, "If Your Presence does not go with us, do not bring us up from here."
>
> —EXODUS 33:14–15

The Hebrew translation for *paniym*, the word used for "My Presence," is "the face (as the part that turns)." *Paniym* is a plural noun.[1] Listen with your heart to what God is telling him. He is saying, "Moses, My faces shall go with you. I will give you manifestations of My grace and goodness through your whole journey. I shall vary My appearance as your necessities require." If that doesn't make you want to shout, I don't know what else to tell you!

> Behold, I send an Angel before you to keep you in the way and to bring you into the place which I have prepared.
>
> —EXODUS 23:20

Don't go anywhere without the presence of God for the journey. The presence of the Lord is so important that as Moses faced his journey, he said to God, "If You don't go with me, I'm not going." If you have His presence, you will have everything you need, but without it, you have nothing.

Moses knew that as God's people—people who had an intimate relationship with God Himself— they should be distinguishable from the people with whom they came into contact who did not know God. He desired for God to make him different from those who did not know God. He said to God, "For how then will it be known that Your people and I have found grace in Your sight, except You go with us? So we shall be separate, Your people and I, from all the people who are upon the face of the earth" (Exod. 33:16).

> ### Don't go anywhere without the presence of God for the journey.

What is it that makes us different? The presence of God is what distinguishes us and sets us apart from everyone else. God understood Moses' request and gave this promise:

> So the LORD said to Moses, "I will also do this thing that you have spoken; for you have found grace in My sight, and I know you by name."
> —EXODUS 33:17

What followed next is the account of Moses' most incredible encounter with God. When Moses found favor with God and received God's promise in verse 17, he went one step further. He took his life in his own hands and asked God for something that no one had ever dared to ask for before:

> And he said, *"Please, show me Your glory."*
> —EXODUS 33:18, EMPHASIS ADDED

Moses doesn't just pray—he begs God for His glory. He says, "Please." Why is Moses' prayer so powerful? Because Moses was willing to pay the price. He was willing to die for it. He wanted God's glory even if it cost him his own life. Think about it. Are you willing to pay the price?

Moses had just gone to a place where no man had gone before. He opened the door to God's glory becoming available to man. Because of his pleading, we can all walk through the door to experience the glory of God. The hunger that God saw in Moses touched His heart, and instead of getting angry, God was moved by His friend. What a great lesson to learn. God hides Himself from the satisfied, but manifests Himself to the hungry. Look at the tenacity of Moses. God begins to present him with other aspects of Himself, but Moses was not satisfied with the things God was offering. (See Exodus 33:19–23.)

"I will make all My goodness pass before you."

That's not what I'm after!

"I will proclaim the name of the Lord before you."

Thanks, but no thanks!

"I will be gracious to you."

Nope!

"I will have compassion on you."

That sounds good, but nope!

Moses was not satisfied with any of those things.

"You cannot see My face; for no man shall see Me, and live."

I know this sounds crazy, but I want to see Your glory!

> And the LORD said, "Here is a place by Me, and you shall stand on the rock. So it shall be, while My glory passes by, that I will put you in the cleft of the rock, and will cover you with

My hand while I pass by. Then I will take away
My hand, and you shall see My back; but My
face shall not be seen."
                    —EXODUS 33:21–23

God gave Moses what he wanted so badly—he
was allowed to get as close as he could to the glory
of God without losing his life.

> The kind of hunger
> that God seeks is not
> a hunger for His
> miracle-working
> power—He seeks
> people who hunger
> for God Himself.

The glory of God has the power to change us. When
Moses came down from the mountain after this
encounter, he was different. His face shone, so much
so that the people were afraid of him. Now you have
to remember that Moses had had many encounters
with God in his life—from the burning bush to all of
the miracles God had done through him. From the
plagues in Egypt and delivering the children of Israel,
to crossing the Red Sea...the daily manna from
heaven and the water from the rock...the cloud by
day and the fire by night...Moses had seen God's miracles and power more than any other human being.
But even Moses knew there was more to God.

When Moses encountered God's glory, it changed
him. His face didn't shine with God's glory when he
parted the Red Sea, but it shone when he longed for
God Himself. The glory of God produces change,
and when God allows you to experience His glory,

those around you will know you are different.

Today many of us settle for a lot less than what
God wants to give us. Miracles are wonderful, and
we certainly need them. But even though God satisfied the hunger of the Israelites with His miraculous
provision of daily manna from heaven, the Israelites
soon despised that manna and forgot the miracle.
The kind of hunger that God seeks is not a hunger
for His miracle-working power—He seeks people
who hunger for God Himself. Only then can we
taste of His glory in our lives.

## The Faith of Moses

God wants to reveal all His goodness to you as a
part of revealing His glory. What was the key ingre-
dient of Moses' hunger for more of God? Moses was
never content with his past experiences. He cried
out for more—something that we as the church desperately need to do. God is a God who loves to
reveal Himself to the hungry, but He will hide from
those who are satisfied and content.

> God came from Teman,
> The Holy One from Mount Paran.
>
> His glory covered the heavens,
> And the earth was full of His praise.
> His brightness was like the light;
> He had rays flashing from His hand,
> *And there His power was hidden.*
>                    —HABAKKUK 3:3–4, EMPHASIS ADDED

"Please show me Your glory." This kind of hunger
in Moses so moved God because it was the greatest

request man had ever asked of God. There is nothing greater for which Moses could ask God.

- It was great faith that filled the heart of Abraham when he stood before the Lord interceding for two cities before God's judgment was about to be executed. (See Genesis 18.)

- It was great faith that filled the heart of Jacob when he wrestled with the angel and said, "I will not let you go until you bless me." (See Genesis 32.)

- It was great faith that filled the heart of Elijah when he prayed that God would rend the heavens, sending down rain. (See 1 Kings 18.)

Moses' prayer for God to send down His glory demonstrated a greater measure of faith than all these examples. Heaven had not heard those words before. It was the greatest request that man could ever ask God: "Please, show me Your glory." Moses stood alone, raising the bar to a level it had never seen before. His request surpassed that of any other man before or after him.

This kind of faith is the highest and greatest level of faith we can ever desire. It was a faith filled with boldness. This was not a faith for getting things from God—it was a faith that believed God's glory could be revealed to him. There is a desperate hunger in my heart to encounter this kind of faith in my life.

Let me share some of the things I learned from studying Moses' life and desire for God. This kind of faith does not come because of confession alone. It doesn't come just because we asked for it on Sunday morning during service. When there is no passion to know Him, our faith is used to getting *things* from God, rather than getting *God's heart and will* for our lives.

## Moses had intimate fellowship with God.

Moses did not ask for God's glory to be revealed without counting the cost. He could ask God because he spent time with God in His presence. It is so important for us to understand that Moses had just spent forty days in God's presence before he asked for God's glory to be revealed. This new relationship with God began with an encounter at the burning bush, when he took off his shoes and stood on holy ground. Holiness must precede the revelation of the glory of God. God spoke face to face with Moses, as a man speaks with his friend.

## Moses received a new revelation of God's grace.

The time Moses spent in God's presence brought a new kind of revelation of God's grace in his life.

> Now therefore, I pray, if I have found grace in Your sight, show me now Your way, that I may know You.
>
> —EXODUS 33:13

Moses was willing to do whatever was necessary to know God. He prayed, "Show me now Your way, that I may know You." Just one chapter earlier, God was so angry with the children of Israel that He was going to wipe them out: "And the LORD said to Moses, 'Go, get down! For your people whom you brought out of the land of Egypt have corrupted themselves'" (Exod. 32:7). I can just imagine Moses standing there thinking, My *people have corrupted themselves? The people I brought out of Egypt?*

God made it very clear to Moses that He was angry with His people. He said:

> "They have made themselves a molded calf, and worshiped it and sacrificed to it, and said, 'This is your god, O Israel, that brought you out of the land of Egypt!'" And the LORD said to Moses, "I have seen this people, and indeed it is a stiff-necked people! Now therefore, let Me alone, that My wrath may burn hot against them and I may consume them. *And I will make of you a great nation.*"
> —EXODUS 32:8–10, EMPHASIS ADDED

God wanted to destroy every single one of the Israelites and make of Moses a great nation. Talk about opportunity knocking on your front door! You would think Moses would be thinking, *What an opportunity to get rid of this stiff-necked gang of complainers.* But no, not Moses. He forgot his own inheritance and was concerned about God's inheritance in them.

> Then Moses pleaded with the LORD his God, and said: "LORD, why does Your wrath burn hot against *Your* people whom *You* have brought out of the land of Egypt with great power and with a mighty hand? *Why should the Egyptians speak, and say, 'He brought them out to harm them, to kill them in the mountains, and to consume them from the face of the earth'?* Turn from Your fierce wrath, and relent from this harm to Your people. Remember

> Abraham, Isaac, and Israel, Your servants, to
> whom You swore by Your own self, and said
> to them, 'I will multiply your descendants as
> the stars of heaven; and all this land that I
> have spoken of I give to your descendants, and
> they shall inherit it forever.'" So the LORD
> relented from the harm which He said He
> would do to His people.
> —EXODUS 32:11–14, EMPHASIS ADDED

There is a brewing in my spirit with each passing
day in the last few months that God is about to touch
us with His glory in a deeper way. The best way to
describe it is like a fountain of joy deep in my heart,
which is beginning to spring up. We are going to see
the goodness of God like never before. My time with
the Lord every day now begins with proclaiming His
goodness being revealed in my life. "I would have lost
heart, unless I had believed that I would see the goodness of the LORD in the land of the living" (Ps. 27:13).

God's goodness is not His glory; it's just the
beginning of God's glory. We sing about it and we
say it, but I believe we are about to experience His
goodness unlike anything we have ever seen. God is
good is His greatest glory.

> Then He said, "I will make *all* my goodness
> pass before you, and I will proclaim the name
> of the LORD before you. I will be gracious to
> whom I will be gracious, and I will have com-
> passion on whom I will have compassion."
> —EXODUS 33:19, EMPHASIS ADDED

His goodness is not complete in the fact that He is
just a good God. God's goodness means God's best,
His beauty, His joy, gladness and welfare concerning

you. This is the time to ask God to enlarge the capacity of our hearts to know Him. Friend, I can't say this enough, "The best is yet to come." God is going to make His goodness known to you just because He is good. The more of our hearts we give to Him, the greater the capacity of our hearts to receive from Him.

> God's goodness is
> not His glory; it's
> just the beginning
> of God's glory.

Moses didn't see a form pass in front of him—*he was granted an audience with God.* It was an audience not with His person, but with a manifestation of God's goodness—the beginning attribute of His glory.

> With the merciful You will show Yourself merciful;
> With a blameless man You will show Yourself blameless;
> With the pure You will show Yourself pure;
> And with the devious You will show Yourself shrewd.
>
> —PSALM 18:25–26

Moses prayed, "Show me Your glory."

God replied, "Moses, I will make all My goodness pass before you." God didn't show Moses His presence, holiness, power or wrath—*He showed His goodness.*

## The Weightiness of God's Glory

Let's look at one last image of God's glory.

In the year that King Uzziah died, I saw the

Lord sitting on a throne, high and lifted up,
and the train of His robe filled the temple.
Above it stood seraphim; each one had six
wings: with two he covered his face, with two
he covered his feet, and with two he flew. And
one cried to another and said:

"Holy, holy, holy is the LORD of hosts;
The whole earth is full of His glory!"

—ISAIAH 6:1–3

The word here for God's glory is *kabod,* and it
means "to make heavy, the weighty presence of
God." We speak of an important person as one who
carries a lot of weight. As the seraphim worship, the
train of the robe of God—His glory—fills the temple, and the posts of the door shake with the weight-
iness, the splendor, the glory of God. What is this
like? How can we envision what is happening here?

Let me help you visualize this scene. *Glory* refers
to the honor, the importance, the weight of a very
powerful person. Imagine yourself standing in the
palace. You have gathered with the royal court and
are in the ballroom of the palace awaiting the
arrival of the king.

At the door stand the royal heralds who
announce the arrival of all the important guests.
Lord and Lady So-and-so arrive. Then Prince and
Princess So-and-so arrive. The hall is filled with an
atmosphere of expectancy and anticipation. Music
has been playing. Guests have been arriving. The
weight of this important occasion can be felt
throughout the room.

Then the heralds blow their trumpets. Suddenly
the atmosphere is charged with electricity. Like the

seraphim, like the angels, like the cloud of witnesses, the heralds announce the arrival of the king. All of the talk...all the preparation...all the building, the decorations, the music have been but a prelude to this moment: the arrival of the king.

The king stands at the door. The doorposts shake. Every head turns; every person bows in reverence and respect. The king has arrived in all his glory. The dance can now begin.

> The dance of true
> worship begins before
> the throne of God.

So it is with our worship. As we worship, a *kairos* moment arrives in which heaven and earth touch. The invisible becomes visible. All flesh has died. We have become living sacrifices. We have repented and died to ourselves. All that matters is seeing the King, greeting the Bridegroom who is about to arrive and dance with His bride.

Now the King welcomes us into His glorious presence and invites us, "Dance with Me." And so the dance of true worship begins before the throne of God. With Bridegroom and bride dancing together, the Father laughs, smiles and rejoices. In that moment, we have kissed the face of God.

## To Kiss God's Face...

1. Receive Jesus. Be clothed in His glory.

2. Ask for His glory to be reflected in your life.

3. Keep your motives pure in your asking.

4. As you worship Jesus, see Him clothing you with His glory.

5. Let His glory change you.

6. In His glorious presence, accept the invitation to the dance.

7. As you dance with Him, kiss His face.

# Chapter 7

# *The* Coming Glory

N ow that you know a little bit about what God's glory is, I want to share with you what I feel God has in store for us in the coming years.

Early one morning I had the most incredible dream. In the dream I saw the most beautiful, plush, deep-green field I had ever seen. The long field was bordered by rolling hills with trees on each side of it. I was in awe of the beauty of the field. In the distance, many people were journeying, not individually, but in groups to the field. They seemed united; like an army marching together, they came.

Suddenly, the field began to glisten with light. I looked up to discover the light's source. It was a cloud of light hovering like a mist over the people. I just stood with all those people, unable to move, looking up into the light. While looking up, I saw cylinders of light beginning to shoot out of the sky onto the people. The light began to cover the people one by one. Each person was covered from head to toe, and, like a tornado, everyone was lifted up and carried into the cloud of light.

I started crying out, "Jesus is coming! Jesus is coming! Could this be the Second Coming of Jesus?"

I heard the Spirit of God say, "Son, this is not the Second Coming. The cylinders of light are My coming glory, which will cover My people. My people are coming to the field, which is rich with My Word, and I will visit My church with My glory again."

## Times of Change Are Coming

As every year draws to a close, I take time in prayer to hear the voice of Holy Spirit about what's coming. I lock myself away for the specific purpose to hear His voice. I ask, "What does God desire to do in my life, in my family and in our church family this coming year?"

I believe we have entered into a time of great changes. Some of these changes will be practical and some will be spiritual in order to get us ready for the coming glory.

As we talked about in the last chapter, the church is coming to a place of personal and corporate hunger for God such as we have never seen. This kind of hunger will be the entryway that will cause God's glory to touch His people. People are becoming more and more dissatisfied with living in their past experiences with God. This hunger will release a new level of God's glory on the earth.

The people are hungry, and church leadership is growing hungrier. Often youth are leading the way with this kind of hunger. Even the little ones want more of God. Many leaders are unsure what to do or where to turn, except to turn to Jesus. No church program they offer can satisfy the people. Just writing about it brings me to tears and makes me long for more of Him in my life.

I'm not sure what this coming glory realm is going to look like. Here is the truth—if I can't even express to you my longing for Him, how in the world can I tell you what this coming glory is going to look like? I do believe that although some of the past outpourings have been good and needed, this coming glory will not be comparable even to the most recent realm.

> No longer are we a generation that seeks His hand. We are a generation that seeks His face.

As I have studied some of the past moves of God, there seems to be a pattern that develops. God moves; the people respond; leaders are equipped; and they get organized. They develop a way and a method to say what happened to them. Then they become a little more skillful and organized, only to become rigid. What ends up happening is that the life of God is quenched, and when God moves in a fresh and new way, many have a hard time moving with God.

The *fuel* of revival is the Word of God.

The *fire* of revival is the Spirit of God.

The *future* of revival is the experience of God's presence.

If not, what often stops the revival is *man, movement, machine, monument.*

This coming glory will take us from being laid out on the floor to walking in the Spirit. No longer are we a generation that seeks His hand. We are a generation that seeks His face. This realm will not be about the manifestations of the Holy Spirit. It will be about *the person* of the Holy Spirit. A place of unprecedented hunger will grow in the hearts of God's people for more of God Himself. It may be a place of uncharted waters to us, but He knows where He's taking us, and He knows how to get us there.

## The Coming Glory Will Change Us

As we learned from Moses, an encounter with God's glory will bring change. God is after you to change you and to make you look like Him.

*Glory* has become a kind of Christian password. People everywhere are talking about the *glory*. Conferences invite people to come and experience the *glory*. More recently there are more songs being written and sung about the *glory*.

But most people avoid what true glory demands, which is *change*. I don't mean to sound arrogant or bitter, but I'm just hungry for the real glory of God. I hunger for the kind of glory that transforms worshipers. When it comes, the services for those who desire to come into His presence will never be the same again. Today, many people go to church, but few go to worship. True worship always results in transformation.

Even though many people are singing and shouting about the glory being poured out, where is the change? If we are truly experiencing the glory of God, why are so few people being healed? Why is the divorce rate in the church higher than it is in the secular world? Why are teens weeping from the wounds they've received from absentee or abusive fathers?

> True worship always results in transformation.

What I'm about to say may seem harsh and judgmental, but there's not an ounce of judgment in my heart. I love God's servants. I know I must not touch God's anointed or do His prophets harm (1 Chron. 16:22). I'm just trying to understand. Across the TV broadcasts, you can hear good preaching, good singing and people shouting about the glory of God. But something is missing. Many preach passionately as they wipe away the sweat. They scream that God has given them a revelation of His glory, but their home lives are in shambles. Why can't the glory about which they preach keep their own marriages together? My heart is troubled for them, and I am praying for them, but something must be wrong.

I must place some of the responsibility on the church. Some sheep would rather have gifting than anointing, charisma instead of character, good preaching instead of integrity. These sheep seem to care little about the heart of the man of God as long as God gives them what they want. They look past issues of character and integrity because "he's a preachin' machine." How sad!

Christian magazines offer full-color ads that fill the pages with slogans like: "The Nation's Premier Praise and Worship Conference," "Come and Experience the

Glory of God" or "Catch the Powerful Presence of [*a famous Christian singer's name*] in Concert." No one will ever be changed in the presence of a singer regardless of how anointed he or she is. No conference ever changes a life. Only an encounter with the pure glory of God will change you.

Hear my heart at this point. I am certainly not out to bash Christian magazines. I am a subscriber and really enjoy them. My point is simply this: *Don't get lost in the hype.* Hype will not change you; good preaching will not change you; great marketing techniques will never change you. Only the true glory of God will change you!

Get ready for *increasing glory.* God loves you so much that each time you step into a new level of glory, He says, "Don't unpack and get comfortable. There is a higher level coming. Don't get used to your surroundings; we are leaving this place soon."

Don't be afraid of change. The course of change in your life will bring brokenness and a dependence on God. All of a sudden, things you trusted in will be stripped from you—no more crutches. I have learned many lessons in my life and ministry. One lesson God has proven in my life over and over again is this: *God will never take something from you without giving you something far greater in return.* The breaking is for the making. So relax, because it's all a part of the process. He is breaking you in order to make you even better.

One of the great joys of my life is playing and coaching ice hockey. I love coaching my sons, Costi and Mikey, and kids who love the game and want to become the best hockey players they can be. I apply this principle in every game and practice. I want the kids to see what they can be rather than what they are.

They may start the season unable to skate backwards, cross over on both sides or shoot the puck hard. This might be the *fact* right now, but the *truth* is that by the end of the season they will all be great. As their coach I can see this, but the fun comes when they begin to see it. They see the *fact* of their lack of skill, but as they practice and work hard, *truth* kicks in, and they begin to believe they can. By the end of the year they're skating backwards, crossing over and burying the puck in the net. (By the way, I asked the Lord if I can have an ice rink in heaven instead of a mansion, so for you hockey buffs, game on!)

God is the greatest coach. He sees the end from the beginning. He doesn't see you unable; He sees you able. He is able to do exceedingly abundantly above all you can ask or think (Eph. 3:20). He is making you into what He wants you to be so that you can do what He has called you to do for His kingdom.

But at the same time, get ready—the enemy will war to keep you in your comfort zone. The minute you experience God's glory and are ready to let Him change you and take you to the next level, the enemy will throw everything at you, including the kitchen sink. But God will see to it that it doesn't knock you out (and He will even buy you a new sink).

What kind of "sinks" will the enemy throw at you? Basically, he attacks with lies since he is the father of lies. Here are some of the lies that Satan

will toss your way in order to stop the changes that
God's glory wants to perform in you:

- You can't go on; you must quit.
- No one suffers like you do.
- You deserve to feel depressed.
- You've earned a pity party.
- It's impossible to recover from this.
- Everyone, especially church people, is against you.
- Don't let anyone know what you're going through. Go it alone.
- The light at the end of the tunnel *is* a train.
- Kill yourself. No one will miss you.

These things are nothing more than distractions.
Distractions are things that keep you in bondage to
what is not important. The antidote to all these lies
is one simple truth:

> And we know that in all things God works for
> the good of those who love him, who have
> been called according to his purpose.
> —ROMANS 8:28, NIV

The key here is "love him." It's time to return to
your first love! Or, to the One who loved you first!

# Returning to Our First Love—His Presence

In order to experience this coming wave of God's

glory, we must first love His presence.

God calls us to return as a church to our first love, His living presence. Major paradigm shifts are taking place in the body of Christ. As we are moving from one level of glory and going to the next, holy dissatisfaction is filling hearts, and people are unsettled with where they are in their walk with God.

> We have lost our way when we chase after His *presents* rather than His *presence*.

We must set our faces toward God as Moses did. God is calling us to a deeper commitment to Him. It's time to leave our old ways behind and be ready to embrace the coming increase of the Holy Spirit. The time has come for all of us to make a deeper commitment to walk toward God.

Returning to our first love will mean...

- Strong commitment to stewardship
- Selfless servant leadership
- Willingness to give of our time and resources to reach the lost
- Deeper intensity and desire for true worship
- Dedication to covenant marriage and healthy, holy families
- Deeper love of God's presence

We've been in a good place, but now holy dissatisfaction is driving us out beyond this place of familiarity. We are leaving our familiar and comfortable zones in church, ministry, worship, prayer, evangelism and fellowship. Something inside us is crying out, "There must be more!"

His presence will be with us for the journey as He promised (Matt. 28:20). We won't have to strive to reach this glorious place; God will reach out to us. We will not work to achieve this place of glory; God will do His work of glory in us.

> And we, who with unveiled faces all reflect the Lord's glory, are being transformed into his likeness with ever-increasing glory, which comes from the Lord, who is the Spirit.
>
> —2 Corinthians 3:18, NIV

# Where Have We Gone Wrong?

We have lost our way when we chase after His *presents* rather than His *presence*. We have gone wrong when our hearts and minds are more on our personal needs instead of worshiping Him. Moses' life taught us that even though he had seen God perform incredible miracles, that did not satisfy his deep hunger for God Himself.

If our time is spent asking Him for answers to our needs and desires, this is not worship, but imitation worship. (Like imitation crab, once you have tasted the real, forget it!) We have missed it when our worship songs become filled with our human needs and not about Him. Like Moses, our motive in seeking God's glory must be pure. Our desire must be for Him and not for what He can do for us.

# What's Coming?

We are living in the most exciting days as believers. We are climbing up the mountain of God, and, like Moses, we are about to have an encounter with God. Joshua went halfway up, but the glory was at the top. We are getting closer, not just in knowing about His glory, but in intimately knowing, encountering and being changed by His glory. This kind of knowing, the *yada* knowledge, is one of the most important Hebrew roots in the Old Testament. It occurs 944 times. A practical definition of *yada* is, "the closest possible intimacy between two persons and the knowledge acquired from such intimacy; a knowledge based on covenant, like a marriage covenant." It's an intimate knowledge of God. It's an experiential knowledge! "Now Adam knew [*yada*] Eve his wife, and she conceived and bore Cain" (Gen. 4:1).

Falling out under the power of God cannot produce this kind of *knowing*. I am not asking, "Do you know about God?" I am asking you, "Do you know God intimately? Are you walking with Him?" I know a lot of people who know a lot of things about God, but very few really know Him. God is taking us higher into the realm of His glory than we have ever been. These will be days of beholding the glory of God.

In late December 2001, I went away for a while to seek the Lord and to hear His voice. Here is a little of what the Lord began to show and speak to my heart about the coming realm called *glory*.

This is a time of preparation and days of getting things in order. We are getting all our things in order because we are leaving where we have been. We will leave this realm that we have become familiar with. This journey is taking us from the Feast of Pentecost and bringing us into the Feast of Tabernacles, and here the Lord will come and be with His people. He will inhabit the praises of His people.

The Lord showed me that we are going to have an "Upper Room experience" all over again—a Day of Pentecost for our time and generation.

Let me comment on a portion of Acts 2 as I share the text with you (italicized type is my commentary):

Now when the Day of Pentecost had fully come, they were all with one accord in one place. And suddenly there came a sound from heaven [*a new sound of worship will fill the church—glory-filled worship*], as of a rushing mighty wind [*a new wind filled the house, and the Holy Spirit filled the people*], and it filled the whole house where they were sitting. Then there appeared to them divided tongues, as of fire, and one sat upon each of them. And they were all filled with the Holy Spirit and began to speak with other tongues, as the Spirit gave them utterance.

—Acts 2:1–4

The upper room was filled with praise, power and strange manifestations. In the coming "upper room" experience, these will be days when the glory of God will be with His people, and the people will fill the buildings with their praises. The desire of the psalmist is emerging:

One thing I have desired of the LORD,
That will I seek:
That I may dwell in the house of the LORD
All the days of my life,
To behold the beauty of the LORD,
And to inquire in His temple.

—PSALM 27:4

O God, You are my God;
Early will I seek You;
My soul thirsts for You;
My flesh longs for You
In a dry and thirsty land
Where there is no water.
So I have looked for You in the sanctuary,
To see Your power and Your glory.

—PSALM 63:1–2

God spoke the following words to my heart:

You are entering into a new realm, and this realm will be new for all of you. This is not a realm that only some have walked in, but where all will walk. I will restore My glory in My church on all those who are hungry for Me. This glory will bring unity to the church and the body of Christ as a whole. These will also be days of grace. The hungry will find grace and favor, for once the glory has been tasted, they will be ruined for ordinary living.

These will be days of *holy dissatisfaction.* Just as Moses cried out, they will be known by their cry, "Please show me Your glory." The cry "Please" will equal the cry for "glory." They will not be content with seeing miracles, though they will see many. They will not be content with fire, though they will experience it. They will not be content

with seeing signs and wonders but will
hunger after Me, and their cry "I want more"
will fill My courts, and I will satisfy them.

In these days I will renew the faith of My
people, and they will see My power at work
in their lives.

The Lord showed me that He is going to release a
supernatural dimension of faith in these days of
hunger. Hunger will release faith, and faith will
release miracles greater than we have never seen.
Get ready! Miracles will become a normal occurrence in your life as you hunger after and keep your
face set God-ward.

The glory of God will be restored to His sanctuary. The *awe* of God will be restored in His house.
The awe of His presence will be restored in a greater
measure to the church.

Our hearts will then echo the passion of the
psalmist, "So I have looked for You in the sanctuary,
to see Your power and Your glory" (Ps. 63:2).

We are coming into this new realm called glory,
and upon our entrance, things will begin to change.
These changes will begin with a tearing down before
a new building begins. Have you ever noticed that it
always takes twice as much effort to tear down than
to build up?

> See, I have this day set you over the nations
>         and over the kingdoms,
> To root out and to pull down,
> To destroy and to throw down,
> To build and to plant.
>                          —JEREMIAH 1:10

God will deal with things like bitterness, offense, anger and rejection because these things belong to your past—they can't come with you. This glory will divide between the clean and unclean.

> ## We are discarding *I-want-from-God* worship and coming into *I-want-God* worship.

*The best is yet to come!* This coming realm of God will release new sounds and smells of worship. Worship is going to sound and look totally different. There will be no need for monthly healing services because healing will take place in every service. People will no longer have to wait for God's servant to touch them because the Holy Spirit will heal them during worship. Instead of bulletins being filled with programs and announcements, they will be filled with the testimony of miracles. Altars will be full during worship as God's power touches the people with miracles. People will not need to be prompted, but they will come to the altar to seek His face and worship Him for who He is.

We are discarding *I-want-from-God* worship and coming into *I-want-God* worship. As God Himself becomes the chief audience of our worship, the revelation of who He is in us will increase. In this place of true worship, the glory and the voice of God are one. It's time to get things in order—and it begins with our personal walk with Christ.

How will we be changed?

- From conference goers to worshipers
- From glory seekers to ones who declare, "Christ in us, the hope of glory"
- From singers to composers of new songs and love songs
- From "gimme" people to givers
- From position hopefuls to servant leaders
- From idolizing Christian stars to glorifying the Creator of the stars
- From wanting manifestations of gold to being refined as pure gold

Are you ready for the coming glory to change you so that you may humbly and intimately come into His presence and kiss His face?

## To Kiss God's Face...

1. Become a living sacrifice ready to be changed by His glory.

2. Set your face God-ward instead of man-ward.

3. Get ready for your own Pentecost.

4. Step outside of your comfort zone into holy dissatisfaction.

5. Let go of offense, bitterness and past hurts.

6. Allow yourself to celebrate the freedom of *I-want-God* worship.

# Chapter 8

# Born Again— Again

O ne morning as I was praying, I asked the Lord how to wind this book down. What is in His heart for the conclusion of this book? It didn't take long for the Holy Spirit to remind me about the day I received Jesus into my heart. In 1974 I gave my heart to Jesus while standing in my brother Benny's room.

Twenty-eight years have passed, but it seems just like yesterday. I was standing at his desk where he studied his Bible. I walked in and sat down at his desk. His Bible was open, and what caught my eye was that it was full of colors. He colored each verse with a different color according to what it meant. Shortly after, he walked in and asked me what I was doing. I told him I was just looking at his Bible, and I asked him why he used all the different colors. He told me about all the colors and their meanings, and then he asked me my life's most important question.

"Sam," he said, "do you want to give your heart to Jesus?"

I replied, "Yes, Benny, I want to give my heart to Jesus." Benny took my hand and led me in the sinner's prayer. When he had finished praying, he asked me to pray, and I said, "Lord Jesus, I ask You to come into my heart and lock Yourself in and throw the key out."

Until this day, it is the greatest prayer that I have ever prayed. Both Benny and I remember it as if it were yesterday.

My brother Benny has touched my life in many ways. Benny's love for Jesus has encouraged me throughout my whole life. It's all about Jesus for him! I have seen his dedication and sacrifice up close, and no matter what comes, he never gives up. Benny is so very dedicated to the Lord. His heart for the hurting is bigger than this whole world. It has been my greatest honor and privilege to serve Jesus with him. He always encourages me by reminding me, "Sam, we all have the same Boss; we do it for Jesus." The greatest gift Benny gave me was on that wonderful day when he took me by the hand and led me to Jesus.

I want to take a moment and say something here to my brother.

> Benny, there are not words to express my heart and love for you. You have said many things to me over the years that have encouraged me in my life and ministry. But without hesitation, the greatest words you have ever spoken to me were those words when I received Jesus into my heart. Benny, thank you for your dedication to the Lord and for the thousand of lives that have been touched by God's love through you.

As I stand in those crusades and see the miracles of people getting healed by the power of God, my heart rings loud with your words, "The greatest miracle is not physical. The greatest miracle is when someone gives their heart to Jesus." Thank you for ministering to the thousands, but thanks for being there for me. Thank you for sharing Jesus with me. Only Jesus knows the impact you have made. It really is the greatest miracle! Benny, I love you with all my heart.

# Jesus Is Coming

The Lord has blessed me with a wonderful family and with all my brothers and sisters. The greatest blessing in this family has been my mother. This godly woman has been our anchor and firm foundation. My mom has dedicated her life to pray for her children and grandchildren. Every morning for hours she prays and asks God to use us all for His glory. In every major crisis she has always been there with a word from the Lord to comfort us. God gave this family a treasure in my mother. Her devotion to the Lord and to us has been our pillar of strength and example. One of things I look forward to every morning is calling her and hearing, often through tears, what the Lord has shown her that morning.

For years, at the end of every phone call I would hear her say, "Son, Jesus is coming soon."

"Yes, Mom," I would agree with her, "Jesus is coming soon."

But in my heart I began to ask myself, *Am I really ready for His coming?* In my heart I really want Him to

come, but then I would think about my wife and my
kids. There are so many things I still want to do with
them. I want to see my kids all grown up and serving
the Lord. I want to grow old with my wife and enjoy
our latter years together. To be very honest, I felt like I
would be short-changed if Jesus came too soon.

One Sunday morning at our church service, a
wonderful servant of God named Fuchsia Pickett
ministered a powerful message. She ministered on
the bride of Christ preparing herself for the
Bridegroom. The presence of God at the end of the
service was so strong. The Lord began to remind me
of what my mom has been saying to me for years:
"Son, Jesus is coming soon; Jesus is coming." Now I
was being confronted by the Holy Spirit about my
putting off His coming. You see, I knew that Jesus
was coming. In my heart I really believed it, but I
had always considered it something that will happen a long time from now. In that moment as
Fuchsia Pickett spoke, I was facing truth: "What if
Jesus came tonight? What if the sky splits open and
Jesus calls me home tonight?"

How about you? When He returns, what condition will He find you in? Are you ready for His
return? In that moment there will be no time to get
things right with those you have hurt. There will be
no time to get your prayer life right. There will be no
time to tell someone you are sorry for being
offended with them.

My friend, there is no greater or more important
question that I can ask you. The time is short. Now
is the time to make things right. Are you living

today as if He may return tonight? Have you put off His coming and in the process lost your devotion for Him today? I encourage you to live every day as if He is coming back tonight. His coming may be sooner than you think.

## Getting Things Right With God

In January 2002, the Lord had called me to an extended fast. I wasn't sure for how long, but I knew the Lord was calling me to it. Early one Tuesday morning shortly after the fast started, I woke up in tears. I had had a dream, and in this dream I saw myself so empty on the inside. In the dream I was crying out, "God, empty me."

> Have you put off His coming and in the process lost your devotion for Him today?

I immediately got up and went into my office. The tears would not stop. I didn't know why I felt so empty. All I knew was that something was going on deep inside me. When I got into my office I could not stop praying and crying out to God, "Empty me; take everything, everything I ever knew of You. I want to know You more right now than ever before; take all the good, all the bad. Fill all that empty space with You. I want to make more room for You, Lord. Thank You for all the things You have done for me in the past, but I want all that I can have of You right now."

## Return; Revive; Restore

In that moment, I gave my heart to Jesus all over again. This time I was sitting at my own desk, with my Bible, and I surrendered everything to Him again. That morning I gave Him my heart, family, ministry, life—everything I had. I opened my Bible and asked the Lord to please confirm what was happening to me and what I saw in the dream from His Word. This passage stared up at me from the pages of my Bible:

> Come, and let us return to the LORD;
> For He has torn, but He will heal us;
> He has stricken, but He will bind us up.
> After two days He will revive us;
> On the third day He will raise us up,
> That we may live in His sight.
> Let us know,
> Let us pursue the knowledge of the LORD.
> His going forth is established as the morning;
> He will come to us like the rain,
> Like the latter and former rain to the earth.
>
> —HOSEA 6:1–3

I was born again, again! My life changed again. This time there wasn't a man there to lead me; it was God calling me into a deeper place with Him. Everything in my relationship with God changed that morning. So here is my encouragement to you: If you want to know Him, it starts by returning to Him.

I am not sure that there is anyone who is totally satisfied with his or her relationship with God. Everything you want, everything you need begins right here: "Come, let us return to the Lord." We have been born again once already, but a greater relationship with God is waiting for you. If you want more of Him, then you must come and return to Him. This is how this great journey begins. You can't know Him until you return to Him.

When you return, bring everything with you— sin, shame, guilt, pain, hurts, offenses. Let Him hear you say, "Father, please forgive me for all these things I've carried in my heart. I want more of You in my life, and these things have been hindrances." Until you deal with these issues, your walk with God will be like a Christian roller coaster. It's time to get off the ride!

> If you want more of Him, then you must come and return to Him.

God promises, "If we confess our sins, He is faithful and just to forgive us our sins and to cleanse us from all unrighteousness" (1 John 1:9).

## "After Two Days He Will Revive Us"

Something on the inside of you will begin to bubble up. A revival has just started. This revival is not at some building, church or city. You don't even have to leave your house. A fountain of life flows deep inside your heart. You return; He revives!

> On the third day He will raise us up,
> That we may live in His sight.
>
> —HOSEA 6:2

Here is the key. God wants you to stay and not just to visit Him. How can you know someone if you are not in that person's presence? He wants you to come up and live in His sight. God told Moses the same thing, "Then the LORD said to Moses, 'Come up to Me on the mountain and be there'" (Exod. 24:12). Moses came to know God on top of the mountain. If you want to experience the glory of God, you have to go up and stay. There is no revelation of glory halfway up. Being close to the top is not close enough! You have to get on up there if you want to know Him. Let's examine this text from Hosea 6 more closely.

> Let us know,
> Let us pursue the knowledge of the LORD.
> His going forth is established as the morning;
> He will come to us like the rain,
> Like the latter and former rain to the earth.
>
> —HOSEA 6:3

In 2 Peter 1:2–4, we read these words:

> Grace and peace be multiplied to you in the knowledge of God and of Jesus our Lord, as His divine power has given to us all things that pertain to life and godliness, through the knowledge of Him who called us by glory and virtue.

When you know Him, grace and peace will fill your life. These are some of the gifts He gives because of knowing Him. Look for the fruit of grace and peace in your relationship with God. If you don't have them, you need to return to Him. Fruit doesn't come because you attend church faithfully or because you listen to worship music while you drive to work. Fruit comes because you really know Him intimately. It's really simple. Look for grace and peace as the evidence of whether or not you are living in His sight.

> ...as His divine power has given *to us all things* that pertain *to life and godliness, through the knowledge of Him* who called us by glory and virtue.
>
> —2 PETER 1:3, EMPHASIS ADDED

Everything relevant to life and godliness comes through the knowledge of Him. If you know Him, you will have everything you need. Because you know Him, you will know His heart and desires. But you can't have these gifts unless you "come, let us return."

> And this is eternal life, that they may know You, the only true God, and Jesus Christ whom You have sent.
>
> —JOHN 17:3

"And this is eternal life"—not just life but intimate life, eternal life. You don't have to die and go to heaven to know Him. You can experience eternal life right now. It begins right here, right now. *Know* means "to perceive, recognize, become acquainted with and understand." Only those who know Him can fully trust Him. When you know Him, He makes His glory known to you.

The apostle Paul, to whom Jesus appeared more than once, was caught up into the third heaven. Paul, who was directly taught by the Lord in the desert and who wrote nearly half the books of the New Testament, knew God as few did. If this man who knew God to this degree says, "That I may know Him and the power of His resurrection, and the fellowship of His suffering, being conformed to His death" (Phil. 3:10), then we certainly need to know Christ more deeply.

If you want to experience the power of the resurrection, be ready for the fellowship of suffering. If you want to know Him as Paul did, be ready to make the same commitment. If you want what Paul wants, be ready to walk where Paul walked.

> But what things were gain to me, these I have counted loss for Christ. Yet indeed I also count all things loss for the excellence of the knowledge of Christ Jesus my Lord, for whom I have suffered the loss of all things, and count them as rubbish, that I may gain Christ and be found in Him.
>
> —PHILIPPIANS 3:7–9

Paul said that to live or die makes no difference to him; "I want to know Jesus!" How many of us are willing to make that kind of decision?

## Look for grace and peace as the evidence of whether or not you are living in His sight.

God makes the promise that when you are intimate with Him, He will come, as surely as the sun rises. He will come to you like the rain. This kind of knowing doesn't happen because you have been at a good service.

"Let us know, let us pursue..." If you want to know Him, you must go after Him.

# Get Close Enough to Kiss His Face

That the God of our Lord Jesus Christ, the
Father of glory, may give to you the spirit of
wisdom and revelation in the knowledge of
Him.

—EPHESIANS 1:17

## The Holy Spirit

The person of the Holy Spirit, who is the spirit of
wisdom, will reveal God to you. The Holy Spirit
knows everything there is to know about God, and
He alone can reveal the heart of the Father because
He comes from the Father. The Holy Spirit who
knows everything has the ability to reveal everything. We need to know the Holy Spirit in order to
know God.

However, when He, the Spirit of truth, has
come, He will guide you into all truth; for He
will not speak on His own authority, but whatever He hears He will speak; and He will tell
you things to come.

—JOHN 16:13

These things I have spoken to you while being
present with you. But the Helper, the Holy
Spirit, whom the Father will send in My name,
He will teach you all things, and bring to your
remembrance all things that I said to you.

—JOHN 14:25–26

*Lord Jesus, thank You for the Holy Spirit.
Wonderful Holy Spirit, open our eyes and reveal
the Father to us; bring us close, real close, so that
we can kiss God's face.*

## Prayer

> For this reason we also, since the day we heard it, do not cease *to pray* for you, and to ask that you may be filled with the knowledge of His will in all wisdom and spiritual understanding; that you may walk worthy of the Lord, fully pleasing Him, being fruitful in every good work and increasing in the *knowledge of God*.
>
> —COLOSSIANS 1:9–10, EMPHASIS ADDED

*Lord Jesus, I pray for a fresh fire of Your Holy Spirit to ignite our worship and prayer, a fresh fire upon our devotion and commitment to live our lives for Your glory alone.*

## Walk with God

> "Now therefore, I pray, if I have found grace in Your sight, show me now Your way, that I may know You and that I may find grace in Your sight. And consider that this nation is Your people." And He said, "My Presence will go with you, and I will give you rest."
>
> —EXODUS 33:13–14

*Lord Jesus, I ask You to fill us with Your presence. Let us hunger after You in true holiness. Fill us with Your glory. May we walk holy and blameless before You.*

## Be still

> Be still, and know that I am God.
>
> —PSALM 46:10

*Know*, *yada*, indicates knowledge based on covenant, an intimate knowledge of God. It's an experiential knowledge! "Be still" means to quit

striving; when you are still and not striving you will
know Him. "He must increase, but I must decrease"
(John 3:30).

> *Lord Jesus, I ask You to teach us how to be still and*
> *to quit striving for our own success. Teach us to*
> *stand and see the salvation of our God. Lord, we*
> *put our trust in You. Now to Him who is able to*
> *do immeasurably more than all we ask or imagine,*
> *according to His power that is at work within us.*
> *We love You, Holy Spirit!*

## Get around the right people

People will either *affect* or *infect* you. So be sure to
surround yourself with people who will take you
into your future and not your past.

> And He Himself gave some to be apostles,
> some prophets, some evangelists, and some
> pastors and teachers, for the equipping of the
> saints for the work of ministry, for the edifying
> of the body of Christ, till we all come to the
> unity of the faith and of the knowledge of the
> Son of God, to a perfect man, to the measure
> of the stature of the fullness of Christ.
>
> —Ephesians 4:11–13

> *Lord, I thank You for all those who serve You with*
> *a pure heart. I pray that godly leaders and mentors*
> *will equip those who desire to be used in Your*
> *kingdom so that Your glory will shine through*
> *them as they touch others.*

## Ask; seek; knock

> So I say to you, ask, and it will be given to you;
> seek, and you will find; knock, and it will be
> opened to you.
>
> —Luke 11:9

Ask for what you desire to have; seek for what you can't see; knock until every hindrance is out of the way.

Ask, Seek, Knock = ASK!

*Lord Jesus, I ask You to tear down every obstacle that stands in the way of answered prayer. Give us Abraham's boldness to stand before You face to face. Father, give us the hungering heart of Moses. Let us never become content or satisfied with just seeing signs and wonders. Lord Jesus, we don't hunger for the miracles—we hunger to talk to You face to face as a man would speak to his friend.*

# Chapter 9

# Kissing *Away* *the* Tears *of* God

A s each day draws to an end, we draw one day closer to the Lord's return. Each passing moment, His desires are increasingly becoming our desires and His passion is invading our hearts. For those who are hungry, God is defining our days with His heart for the lost. Every experience with Jesus is only meant to get us closer to His heart. I believe true revival begins when the Great Commission becomes our mission.

My heart is flooded with emotion, and with each experience come a greater love and longing for more of Him in my life. I don't know why He keeps doing these things in my life, except to allow my life to be a blessing and encouragement to others. The same God who has touched my life will touch your life. He is not a respecter of persons.

I know this one thing: It is a privilege to serve Him. Serving Him is the greatest honor any of us can ever experience. My life has been a process of walking with God as the Holy Spirit goes deeper and deeper in my heart with God's desire and plan for my life.

> But as it is written:

> "Eye has not seen, nor ear heard,
> Nor have entered into the heart of man
> The things which God has prepared for those
>     who love Him."
>                                   —1 CORINTHIANS 2:9

A recent experience was the most defining and heartbreaking step I have taken in my walk with the Lord. Have you ever felt like just quitting? Well, that's exactly the place where I had come to in my life. Not to a place of giving up on my life, ministry or family, but I came to this point in my walk with the Lord. I love ministering to Him and to His people, but I was so empty inside. I had never felt this emptiness before in my life, and I did everything I knew to do. I was faithful to worship, but no answer. I fasted and prayed, and still no answer. At every opportunity, I would go to the altar with a pure heart and cry out to God, "Please, just show me…tell me…why do I feel so empty on the inside?"

I had never felt this kind of emptiness before. I didn't want to quit, because you can't quit the ministry. But I felt that if this is all there is to going to church and being in the ministry, I wanted out. I felt that I could minister just as effectively working at 7-Eleven or coaching hockey. I knew there must be more to God, but I wanted to know, "What is this missing piece in my heart?"

## God's Heart for the Lost

One morning as I prayed a few months ago, the Lord asked me a question, one I have never heard Him ask me before. He said, "Do you want Me to give you faith to call those things that are not as though they were, or do you want Me to give you faith to tell people about Me?" This question not only changed my life...again, but it also shook me. I knew the choice was mine to make. As I pondered the importance of this question, I felt the weight of it on my heart. It seemed minutes passed, but in a few seconds I said, "Lord, I want faith to tell people about You."

The moment the words were out of my mouth, the very foundation of my life was shaken, an experience that is difficult to explain even now. A well of tears opened deep inside me. I have shed more tears in the past few months for the lost than all the tears I'd shed prior to that put together.

> "Lord, I want faith to tell people about You."

The next morning a man to whom I had not spoken in about three years called me on my cell phone. He didn't know the Lord, and he was going through a very difficult time in his life. I had no idea how he even knew my phone number. He asked if we could meet right away, saying, "I don't know who else to talk to about this, and I trust you."

We met for a short time over a cup of coffee. He said to me, "I have watched you for years. I've watched you around your kids, your family, and I can tell that you're a real Christian." He opened his heart and shared what he was going through with his family. His world was falling apart. I started to share with him about how much Jesus loves him, and tears began to fill his eyes as I just shared the love of Jesus with him.

In my head I was already planning what to tell him: "Look…this is where you messed up, here are the steps to making things right." But I just couldn't get those words out. I knew this was not the time to dissect his situation and give him steps one, two and three. This was my moment to share with him about his greatest need—a personal relationship with Jesus. I prayed with him to receive Jesus and gave him instructions in walking with God.

When I left him and returned to my car, I started to cry, not knowing exactly why. I stayed in the car a little while praying and trying to get my composure back. I asked the Lord, "Why is my heart troubled?"

## I can tell them about Jesus and His love for them. It was the jewel that had been missing in my life.

The Lord reminded me about one specific situation that arose while this man was sharing his pain with me. "You almost missed it," the Lord told me. "While he was telling you about his pain, you were thinking about what to say to him."

Immediately I asked the Lord to forgive me and give me His heart for the lost. Over the past few months I have learned that everyone with whom we come into contact wants to be loved—especially those who don't know Jesus. The Lord's heart is to reach the lost. So many need to be rescued from the grips of hell. The greatest calling on your life and mine is to be a soulwinner just as Jesus was.

This experience helped me to understand that it's all about souls! This is what had been missing in my worship. This revelation helped me to define why I worship. This is what had been missing when I preached the Word of God, which I love. It's the reason I love to minister to people. I can tell them about Jesus and His love for them. It was the jewel that had been missing in my life.

The purpose of gathering is not for show or to boast about how many meetings you've attended, how many people have been healed because you prayed for them or how many gold flakes are shimmering on your face. The purpose for gathering is to reach the lost for Jesus. Since God birthed this revelation deep into my spirit, I must be very honest with you; my heart has been so frustrated with all the revival junkies who spend their life running from one revival service to another. They go from river to river, stream to stream, puddle to puddle and, yes, church to church. These junkies (not all) chase after signs and prophecy, this river and that river. They love to defend their point of view. That's OK, but many of them can't remember the last time they led someone to Jesus.

## Revival and Evangelism

When the Lord returns, He is coming back for an End-Time harvest—not an End-Time revival. The church will be in harvest mode, not in revival mode.

*Revival* is to revive something that once lived and had life. You can't revive what has never lived. Revival is for Christians who have accepted Christ as Savior but have lost the fire and become lukewarm in their relationships with Him. These are the ones who need to be revived! Inside the church building is where revival happens. It is a place where people get empowered with the Holy Spirit.

Outside the church building is for evangelism. *Evangelism* is giving new life to those who are dead in their trespasses and sins. These people have never had the life of God before. "And you He made alive, who were dead in trespasses and sins" (Eph. 2:1).

## The Lord Never Called Us to Stay in the Upper Room

Some people have been in the upper room for years and have missed so many opportunities to share Jesus with the hurting. While people are going to hell, maybe even their own family members, they are still laid out on the floor or chasing the next move of God. (Sorry to be so blunt.)

If we don't go out
and take the harvest,
then the upper room
is all in vain.

I am not saying that you should not enjoy the upper room, *but at some point you have to come out.* The disciples didn't stay. They received God's power, then took it to the streets. Moses didn't stay up on the top of the mountain after he encountered the glory of God. He marched right back down and ministered to the people.

This is not the time for us to stay in the upper room. We must go out and reap the harvest, which is plentiful. There is a work to be done for the Lord. If we don't go out and take the harvest, then the upper room is all in vain.

Do you realize you are about to see the greatest harvest of souls being saved? The Lord is going to raise you up as a laborer in this harvest. You will see your family, your friends, coworkers and even your mean boss getting saved. Don't count anybody out! It's time to get out of the upper room and share the love of Jesus with everybody everywhere. It's harvest time!

> Believe on the Lord Jesus Christ, and you will
> be saved, you and your household.
>
> —Acts 16:31

It is time to reap the harvest!

As we worshiped during a recent Sunday morning service, the Lord allowed me to see something in a quick vision concerning the lost. I saw a row of doors in a straight line. On each door there was a sign. The signs read, "Blessings," "Prosperity," "Wealth," "Riches," "Faith," "Healing" and "Favor." In front of each door stood thousands of people. Some were yelling for the doors to open. Some were shaking their fists and reciting Scripture, commanding the doors to open. Others were praying and crying as they begged the doors to open. Others prophesied. But not one of the doors opened.

The Lord spoke to my heart and said, "Behind these doors are untold blessings, blessings like they have never seen before. But I want you to tell them that these doors will not open until they have my heart for the lost. When they touch My heart with the lost, I will touch their heart with My blessings." The moment God gives you His heart—not just *a* heart for the lost, but *His* heart for the lost—He is setting you up to see His blessings and to walk in them, *all of them*!

The greatest presence and anointing of God you will ever feel is when you are leading someone to Jesus. It is the greatest privilege He has given us. We spend a lot of time in our Christian life studying, praying, worshiping and fellowshiping, but how much of our time is spent sharing Jesus with others? The Great Commission must become our mission.

That morning I put a challenge before our church body. There are 168 hours in a week. I asked the congregation to give one hour a week, or ten minutes a day, to the Great Commission. It only takes one hour a week to share the love of Jesus with hurting people. The congregation accepted my challenge, and the people in our church are seeing incredible things happen as people get saved and healed as a result of their efforts.

## Awakened to Witness

Let's take a quick journey through God's Word and allow His Word to inspire you. The reason I love telling people about Jesus is because Jesus is my motivation.

> But God demonstrates His own love toward us, in that while we were still sinners, Christ died for us. Much more then, having now been justified by His blood, we shall be saved from wrath through Him.
>
> —ROMANS 5:8–9

How can I not tell them about God's love? The heartbeat of God is what moves me to tell them.

### Man is lost without Jesus.

Jesus came to seek and save that which was lost. He was continually seeking out the hurting, afflicted and tormented. He had one goal for His life—He came to redeem mankind to Himself. Jesus came to save people. This was His first and last mission. He told the first group of men, "Follow Me, and I will make you fishers of men" (Matt. 4:19).

> The greatest presence and anointing of God you will ever feel is when you are leading someone to Jesus.

The next time you go to the grocery store, notice the person at the checkout counter or the young man wheeling your cart to the car. When we see that these people are lost for eternity without Jesus, I think things will change. The only hope for mankind is understanding who Jesus is and what He has done for us on the cross. Can you imagine what it would be like standing in heaven with Jesus, and just outside the gate you notice familiar faces looking at you and screaming, "You knew and never

told me? Why didn't you tell me about Jesus?"
(Read Luke 16:19–31.)

## The cross—God's love on display

The cross is where we see God's wrath and love
come together. There Jesus took God's wrath on
Himself because He loved us. When you realize just
how much He loves the world, everything you do
takes a back seat to evangelism.

## Miracles are to be a sign to the lost.

Miracles are a sign to the unbeliever that Jesus is
alive.

> But Peter said, "We don't have any money for
> you! But I'll give you something else! I com-
> mand you in the name of Jesus Christ of
> Nazareth, *walk!*" Then Peter took the lame man
> by the hand and pulled him to his feet. And as
> he did, the man's feet and ankle-bones were
> healed and strengthened so that he came up
> with a leap, stood there a moment and began
> walking! Then, walking, leaping, and praising
> God, he went into the Temple with them.
>
> —ACTS 3:6–8, TLB

Some of the greatest miracles should be happening on the streets—not at a special healing service
on a Sunday night. People shouldn't have to wait
for a Sunday service or a Wednesday night Bible
study service to receive their healing. Miracles
should be a part of every believer's everyday life.

> And they went out and preached everywhere,
> the Lord working with them and confirming the
> word through the accompanying signs. Amen.
>
> —MARK 16:20

> Therefore they stayed there a long time, speaking boldly in the Lord, who was bearing witness to the word of His grace, granting signs and wonders to be done by their hands.
>
> —ACTS 14:3

Philip preached in Samaria, and the result was that when the people witnessed the miracles that happened, the entire city was turned upside down for God.

> Then Philip went down to the city of Samaria and preached Christ to them. And the multitudes with one accord heeded the things spoken by Philip, hearing and seeing the miracles which he did. For unclean spirits, crying with a loud voice, came out of many who were possessed; and many who were paralyzed and lame were healed. And there was great joy in that city.
>
> —ACTS 8:5–8

## Seeing the needs of others

It is unlikely that people without Jesus are going to show up unannounced at your front door and say, "Can I go with you to church today?" They won't be knocking on your door asking you to pray for them. The truth is that you may never hear from them, even though they live right next door. We can easily ignore them and forget that they are in desperate need of a Savior.

Luke 16 tells us the story of the rich man who went to hell. In this parable, we learn that it wasn't the fact that this man had money or wore fine clothes that upset God—it was because he did not care for the needs of others. God had a problem with the rich man because that man never saw the beggar who sat outside his gate when he lived on earth. The beggar died and went to heaven, and the rich man died, tormented, to spend eternity in hell (Luke 16:19–31).

We must desire to
bring as many people
with us to heaven as
we can. How could
we do anything less?

We have a far greater wealth than all the riches in this world. We have been blessed with "every spiritual blessing in the heavenly places in Christ" (Eph. 1:3). We need to share the wealth we have received with our family, friends, neighbors and fellow workers. Be careful not to become so focused on the "bless me" experience that you don't notice the spiritual beggar at your gate. (See Luke 16:19–31.)

## God Desires That All Be Saved

The Lord desires that everyone be saved, no matter what we think of them. The important lesson from the Great Commission is simple: We must desire to bring as many people with us to heaven as we can. How could we do anything less?

I want to hear Jesus say, "Well done!"

> His lord said to him, "Well done, good and faithful servant; you were faithful over a few things, I will make you ruler over many things. Enter into the joy of your lord."
>
> —Matthew 25:21

If I ignore the Great Commission, yes, I will make it to heaven. But I should not expect a great reward. To please Jesus must become our greatest desire. Will you give one hour a week—ten minutes a day—to influence others with the love of Jesus? Do it because you love Jesus. Do it for people who are going to hell unless someone tells them about His love for them. Do it for people whose only hope is to hear the gospel.

> The Lord is not slack concerning His promise, as some count slackness, but is longsuffering toward us, not willing that any should perish but that all should come to repentance.
>
> —2 PETER 3:9

If we don't tell them, how will they come to know Him? Every time a lost soul comes to the Lord, we wipe one more tear away from God's face.

# Chapter 10

# Created *to* Worship

ot long ago, I gave this manuscript to my editor thinking that I was done and that the book was finally finished. My wife and kids kidnapped me, confiscated my cell phone and computer, and we took off to the beach for a much-needed vacation. My wife and children wanted their daddy back. We had a great time together.

However, the first night as we settled down to sleep, a stirring began in my heart. I knew the Lord was dealing with my heart about something, but what was it? During the night this stirring would not let up, but only intensified. So I got up and began to pray, asking the Lord, "What is this about?"

The Holy Spirit spoke quietly to my heart and said, "You are not done writing. There is one more chapter I want you to write. Tell them about worshiping Jesus, and close the book encouraging them that *the best is yet to come.*"

The reason I wrote this book is simple. It's not to

get my name out there or to have a best-selling book. The *only* reason is to encourage you in your walk with the Lord Jesus. It is my prayer that God would use this book to encourage you to stay hungry for Him. No matter what you are going through right now, the Lord is stirring my heart to let you know...

### the BEST is yet to come!

# You Were Created to Worship God

But the hour is coming, and now is, when the true worshipers will worship the Father in spirit and truth; for the Father is seeking such to worship Him.

—JOHN 4:23

Did you notice that Jesus said that it's not a matter of *when* you worship but *whom* you worship? "True worshipers will worship the Father in spirit and truth." Until we worship the true and living God in the power of the Holy Spirit, we have forfeited the fundamental purpose of our own existence, and we vainly worship the god of this world.

If we don't worship the true and living God with the power of the Holy Spirit, then we will worship the god of this world with his evil and counterfeit spirits. This is why the greatest war you will ever fight is the war of worship. God created you to worship Him in spirit and truth, but Satan wants you to worship him with his counterfeit spirits.

### False worship

Satan said, "I will be like God."

For you have said in your heart:
"I will ascend into heaven,
I will exalt my throne above the stars of God;
I will also sit on the mount of the congrega-
      tion
On the farthest sides of the north;
I will ascend above the heights of the clouds,
I will be like the Most High."

—Isaiah 14:13–14

The enemy fights for your worship. From the very beginning he wanted to be God and to be worshiped as God. Real worship belongs to God. All the enemy can offer is imitation worship. Satan could never be God, but he desired to be worshiped like God, so he set up a complete imitation.

## True worship

Let me explain. You were created to worship God, but until you came to know Jesus as your personal Savior, your heart was filled with imitation forms of worship. According to Christian philosopher and mathematician Blaise Pascal, within all of us is a God-shaped void.

Have you ever pieced together a jigsaw puzzle? Did you ever have an empty place and find a piece that looked just perfect to fill that spot? But try as you could…force it with all your might…the piece that looked right just wouldn't fit into the spot you wanted it to fill. Nothing could fill that empty place except the *right piece of the puzzle.*

Only the true, living God revealed in Jesus Christ can fill the God-shaped void in our lives. True worship only happens when our empty lives are filled by the Spirit of the living God.

Today, people try to fill this God-shaped void with all sorts of imitation worship, such as entertainment, self-image, worldly possessions, music, career or money. Just watch television, and you will see that advertisers are aware that people will worship *anything*. Advertisers fill the airwaves with commercials and infomercials about making you look and feel good. They try to convince you that you can't be happy with the way you look or feel until you buy their product. It's all designed to get you to buy this or that. Advertisers have come up with every imaginable gadget and gimmick from diet pills to "Ab" machines, from belts to exercise machines, all to help you look better.

> True worship only happens when our empty lives are filled by the Spirit of the living God.

False worship is all about looking and feeling good. Imitation worship is all about you looking good. But false worship will never satisfy or fill the emptiness of lonely hearts without Jesus. It's important to exercise, eat well and live a long life. Yet the purpose of our existence is not to be measured by how much body fat we have. Even the healthiest can die in a tragic unexpected situation; without Jesus, what does it matter?

We were born to die, and every one of us will die once—and then the judgment. But Jesus died for us not only to live a long life here on earth, but also to live forever with Him. (In heaven we won't be counting calories or running on the treadmill. Hallelujah!)

## What Was Worship Like Before the Fall?

Have you ever wondered what worship must have been like before the Fall? There are only two main passages of Scripture that describe the origin and fall of Lucifer—Ezekiel 28:1–19 and Isaiah 14:2–23. Let's look at the relationship between these two passages.

In Isaiah, we learn that Lucifer is heaven's fallen worship leader.

> Your pomp is brought down to Sheol,
> And the sound of your stringed instruments;
> The maggot is spread under you,
> And worms cover you.
> How you are fallen from heaven,
> O Lucifer, son of the morning!
> How you are cut down to the ground,
> You who weakened the nations!
> For you have said in your heart:
> "I will ascend into heaven,
> I will exalt my throne above the stars of God;
> I will also sit on the mount of the congrega-
>         tion
> On the farthest sides of the north;
> I will ascend above the heights of the clouds,
> I will be like the Most High."
> Yet you shall be brought down to Sheol;
> To the lowest depths of the Pit.
> —Isaiah 14:11–15

Ezekiel goes on to describe Lucifer:

Moreover the word of the LORD came to me,
saying, "Son of man, take up a lamentation
for the king of Tyre, and say to him, 'Thus says
the Lord GOD:

"You were the seal of perfection,
Full of wisdom and perfect in beauty.
You were in Eden, the garden of God;
Every precious stone was your covering:
The sardius, topaz, and diamond,
Beryl, onyx, and jasper,
Sapphire, turquoise, and emerald with gold.
The workmanship of your timbrels and pipes
Was prepared for you on the day you were cre-
      ated.

"You were the anointed cherub who covers;
I established you;
You were on the holy mountain of God;
You walked back and forth in the midst of
      fiery stones.
You were perfect in your ways from the day
      you were created,
Till iniquity was found in you.

"By the abundance of your trading
You became filled with violence within,
And you sinned;
Therefore I cast you as a profane thing
Out of the mountain of God;
And I destroyed you, O covering cherub,
From the midst of the fiery stones."
                                    —EZEKIEL 28:11–16

The descriptive language used here of the king of
Tyre and the king of Babylon goes beyond what
could be applied to any earthly kings or rulers and
points to the king behind the kings who reigned. In

these two main scriptures, we see a description of Satan before his fall.

Many theologians believe that Satan's fall took place before the Creation of man, and he was cast out of the presence of God. They propose that Satan's fall is what caused the earth to go into a chaotic condition as seen in Genesis 1:1–2: "In the beginning God created the heavens and the earth. The earth was without form, and void; and darkness was on the face of the deep. And the Spirit of God was hovering over the face of the waters." The argument is that God created the earth perfect, and that between verse one and two something must have happened to cause the earth to go from perfection to total chaos. Lucifer's fall was that *something*.

He was called *Lucifer*, which means "daystar or light bearer." "And no wonder! For Satan himself transforms [disguises] himself into an angel of light" (2 Cor. 11:14). Lucifer was the chief musician of heaven and led all the worship there.

Lucifer was heaven's light bearer. Imagine the glory and all the colors that would fill the heavens as God's glory—the very light of His being, His iridescent light and color—would fill the heavens with splendid rays of light. God's glory would hit Lucifer, and, like a mirror, he would reflect the glorious colors and light, which would then fill the heavens. This is why he was called a "light bearer."

Lucifer was the anointed cherub who covered the throne and was consecrated to the Lord. He saw himself as a guardian angel that protects, much like a high priest protected the temple of God (Ezek. 28:14–15).

He was in Eden, the garden of God (Ezek. 28:13). Lucifer came to Eve and Adam in the form of a serpent to rob them of their relationship with God.

He was in the holy mountain (or kingdom) of God on the sides of the north. *The Mountain of God* speaks of worship (Ezek. 28:14; Ps. 48:1). This is a very important understanding to which I will refer again later in this chapter.

He was decked with precious stones set in gold. Imagine the brilliance of these beautiful colors— the sardius, topaz, diamond, beryl, onyx, jasper, sapphire, turquoise and emerald set in gold. As God's glory and light would hit him, all these stones and colors would illuminate and reflect off his breastplate.

> ### Lucifer was heaven's worship leader and fallen musician, created with music in his being.

From the beginning, God's desire was for Lucifer to be clothed with a "coat of light" to reflect and illuminate the glory of God. It was the glory from the throne of God that gave light to Lucifer when he was in heaven.

Joseph received a coat of color from his father, Jacob (Israel), as a gift.

> Now Israel loved Joseph more than all his children, because he was the son of his old age. Also he made him a tunic of many colors.
>
> —GENESIS 37:3

Joseph was his father's favorite son, and his father

made for him a royal coat with long, flowing sleeves, which set him out as the favored one. His father, Jacob, had chosen Joseph to be the one through whom the divine blessings would flow. (I hope you are getting the picture of how much God loves you.) Just as Jacob proclaimed his affection to his son Joseph by dressing him up with a coat of many colors, signifying his father's honor, God, your heavenly Father, wants to dress you up with His coat of many colors so that His anointing will be reflected in and through your life. This is the Father's gift to you! We are going to shine like never before.

Lucifer was heaven's worship leader and fallen musician, created with music in his being. "The workmanship of your timbrels and pipes was prepared for you on the day you were created" (Ezek. 28:13).

These instruments were marks of joy. Much of the "music" that is being sung now is far from being joyous. When Lucifer was created, within his very being was created the sound of instruments. He didn't stand in heaven with a guitar in his hands or sit behind the keys of a piano to make music. *He was the instrument.* Every sound was created in him as part of his voice and music. Every time he breathed, he breathed the sound of musical notes! (See Isaiah 14:11.)

Lucifer walked in the midst of the fiery stones. "You were on the holy mountain of God; you walked back and forth in the midst of fiery stones" (Ezek. 28:14). My understanding when I studied this is that when he walked back and forth in the midst of the fiery stones, these were not just stones, but flashing jewels of light that would shoot up from beneath him as he walked. As he attended to the presence of God, these stones of fire would glitter and sparkle like fire beneath him.

God created Lucifer to be...

- Heaven's light bearer
- The anointed cherub who covers
- The one who covered the throne of God in Eden
- On the holy mountain of God
- Decked out with stones set in gold
- Heaven's musician

In Genesis 1:2, the earth is described as being "without form, and void; and darkness was on the face of the deep." In verse 3 we read: "Then God said, 'Let there be light'; and there was light." This light was not the light of the sun or moon, because God did not create the sun, moon and stars until the fourth day (Gen. 1:14–18).

> God *is* light. He is not a light—God is light's source.

What was this light that brought order to what was only chaos? I believe this light was God's iridescent light and glory being revealed in the earth. God simply released who and what He is, and the light of His glory was manifested. Everything that was out of order came back into order and restoration. But that's not all! The day He said, "Let there be light," a new sound of music filled the earth. Music was released as the sounds of heaven filled the earth.

Light is one of the most astonishing productions

of God's power. It is the way that all His works are discovered, because God is light and in Him is no darkness. In the New Testament, we read this:

> Every good gift and every perfect gift is from above, and comes down from the Father of lights, with whom there is no variation or shadow of turning.
>
> —JAMES 1:17

When God turns, there is no shadow of turning. This means that when God turns around or moves, there is no shadow to be found because He is light. God *is* light. He is not a light—God is light's source. "This is the message which we have heard from Him and declare to you, that God is light and in Him is no darkness at all" (1 John 1:5).

## The Light of Worship

There are many details of God's creativity that our finite minds cannot comprehend. For example, if "natural light" travels at 186,000 miles per second, how fast does God's light travel? How could plants live on the third day of Creation, before the sun was created? What light existed before the sun, and what light source did God use to mark the first three days?

Physicists and scientists have explained that light travels through space at a speed of 186,000 miles per second. As light travels at that speed, it rides on electromagnetic waves or "radio waves." As this light travels through space it has a threshold of audibility, which can be heard as notes or tones. Science has proven the connection between light and music. They are the same thing—just on different frequencies in the light spectrum.[1]

As human beings we can only see and hear 3 percent of the entire light spectrum of the universe. Now think about it; 97 percent of all light and sound in the spectrum of light we do not see, hear or understand. But just because you don't see or hear it doesn't mean it does not exist. Dogs hear at a frequency that we humans can't hear. Dolphins in the sea hear sound frequencies we could never detect without instruments. When God said, "Let there be light," He not only revealed His glory, but He also released music and a new sound in the earth.

If human beings see only 3 percent of the entire light spectrum, what would we see if God readjusted our human visibility to 70 percent or 80 percent? The way we approach worship would be totally different. We would never worship God the same way ever again. I doubt whether we would interrupt times of corporate worship to give announcements! Imagine what worship would be like if you could see all the colors in the light spectrum. As the service begins in the house of God, and the instruments begin to play and the worship team starts to minister to the Lord, it would be the greatest light show ever.

Remember that just because you don't see it doesn't mean it doesn't exist. Worship would go to a whole new level. God's people would lift their voices together with the instruments, and the heavens above us would light up with colors of praise and worship. (They do this already; we just don't see it.)

All the Levites who were musicians—Asaph,

Heman, Jeduthun and their sons and relatives—stood on the east side of the altar, dressed in fine linen and playing cymbals, harps and lyres. They were accompanied by 120 priests sounding trumpets. The trumpeters and singers joined in unison, as with one voice, to give praise and thanks to the LORD. Accompanied by trumpets, cymbals and other instruments, they raised their voices in praise to the LORD and sang:

"He is good;
    his love endures forever."

Then the temple of the LORD was filled with a cloud, and the priests could not perform their service because of the cloud, for the glory of the LORD filled the temple of God.

—2 CHRONICLES 5:12–14, NIV

The best is yet to come!

# What Happens in Worship That We Do Not See?

When the enemy lost his position, God removed him out of His immediate presence forever. Now this place belongs no longer to Lucifer—it belongs to us. God created a people for Himself, and now He will inhabit their praises. This is why the greatest war you will fight is the war of worship. The enemy hates it when you worship God. It brings back bad memories of the place and position he once held. (Please read Psalm 102:12–28; it will bless you.)

The apostle Paul said in Ephesians 6:12, "For we do not wrestle against flesh and blood, but against principalities, against powers, against the rulers of the darkness of this age, against spiritual hosts of wickedness in the heavenly places."

Where are these spirits of darkness? They are above you. These wicked spirits fight you to keep you from worshiping God. The only thing that can disperse the darkness *is light*. As you worship God in spirit and truth, your worship goes before God and the enemy as light, breaking through the darkness from the enemy and his spirits of darkness. Jesus said, "You are the light of the world. A city that is set on a hill cannot be hidden" (Matt. 5:14). In His great act of Creation, light was God's answer to the dominance of darkness. And every time you and I begin to worship God, although we don't see it, His light is shattering the darkness above us.

> For it is the God who commanded light to shine out of darkness, who has shone in our hearts to give the light of the knowledge of the glory of God in the face of Jesus Christ.
> —2 CORINTHIANS 4:6

> In Him was life, and the life was the light of men. And the light shines in the darkness, and the darkness did not comprehend it.
> —JOHN 1:4–5

Science confirms God's Word with discoveries about music and sound. Not long ago I was reading an article titled, "Sound Waves May Offer Noninvasive Tumor Cure." The article was about the removal of cancerous tumors in a tube-like machine with ultrasound waves beamed deep into the cancerous area. Little bursts of heat signaled beams to cook the tumor to death without cutting the skin.[2] There is more scientific evidence. Science is making discoveries about "the equivalent sounds for colors."

If God could let us see just a little more, we would see a light show millions...trillions...of times more spectacular than anything we see with our finite vision.

Music was David's access to the presence of God. "And to the angel of the church in Philadelphia write, 'These things says He who is holy, He who is true, "He who has the key of David, He who opens and no one shuts, and shuts and no one opens"'" (Rev. 3:7).

In a music scale there are seven tones, just as there are seven major colors in the light spectrum. Researchers have discovered that the Spectro-Chrome frequency for the color *red* is the same in music as for the musical note G. Each musical note frequency has a color frequency in the light spectrum, so each note on the keyboard has a different color.

Imagine the colors of music as worship fills God's house when the pianist starts playing. Not just one note but chords, and now the guitarist, drummer, saxophonist and all the instruments join in. If God could let us see just a little more, what colors, what prisms of light, would we see in worship? We would see a light show millions...trillions...of times more spectacular than anything we see with our finite vision.[3]

He has put a new song in my mouth—
Praise to our God;
Many will see it and fear,
And will trust in the LORD.

—PSALM 40:3

# The Holy Mountain of God

Mountains in the Word of God often refer to places of worship. Lucifer once stood on the holy mountain of God, but he was cast out as a profane thing because of his rebellion (Ezek. 28:16).

When Jesus dwelled on earth, He had an encounter with Satan on a mountaintop—and the issue was worship.

> Again, the devil took Him up on an exceedingly high mountain, and showed Him all the kingdoms of the world and their glory. And he said to Him, "All these things I will give You if You will fall down and worship me." Then Jesus said to him, "Away with you, Satan! For it is written, 'You shall worship the LORD your God, and Him only you shall serve.'" Then the devil left Him, and behold, angels came and ministered to Him.
>
> —MATTHEW 4:8–11

Satan so desperately wanted to make a deal with Jesus. If Jesus would just worship him, he would give Jesus all the kingdoms of the world and their glory. This last wilderness temptation was all about worship, because worship wins the nations. Counterfeit worship robs the nations of true evangelism. From the beginning, Satan wanted to be worshiped in the same way he had seen God being worshiped.

God is calling us to come higher up the mountain to worship. The first place where worship is mentioned in the Bible is connected with Abraham going up the mountain to put his son Isaac on the altar (Gen. 22:5). The call of God to us all is to come higher. How high up the mountain you go is up to you. You choose the elevation. You determine how high in God you want to go.

> Now it shall come to pass in the latter days
> That the mountain of the LORD's house
> Shall be established on the top of the mountains,
> And shall be exalted above the hills;
> And peoples shall flow to it.
> Many nations shall come and say,
> "Come, and let us go up to the mountain of
> the LORD,
> To the house of the God of Jacob;
> He will teach us His ways,
> And we shall walk in His paths."
> For out of Zion the law shall go forth,
> And the word of the LORD from Jerusalem.
> —MICAH 4:1–2

## How to Face and Handle Tough Situations

When difficulties come, they come for one reason— to keep you from going up the mountain to worship God. The enemy wants to keep you beneath the weight of the difficulties. He does not want you going up the mountain, because once you begin to worship God, you begin to ascend over your problems.

Have you ever noticed that situations look so big

when looking from the bottom of the mountain, but they look so small from a vantage point of standing on the top and looking down the mountain? When you have climbed up the mountain of worship, you get caught up with God's greatness and just how big God is. While you are on the journey to the top, you actually transcend your problem by ascending in the presence of God. It's similar to flying in an airplane—from 35,000 feet above earth, things look very small.

Mountains not only speak of worship; they also speak of a high place in God. It was on a mountain when Jesus was transfigured before His disciples (Matt. 17:1–2). There is a place on the mountain of worship where even the enemy cannot touch you. There is a path, a place to God, "that path no bird knows, nor has the falcon's eye seen it. The proud lions have not trodden it, nor has the fierce lion passed over it" (Job 28:7–8).

In Scripture, the Word is speaking of Satan and his evil spirits when it speaks of birds, falcons, vultures and fierce lions. There is a place where none of these things can touch you. We are protected through the blood of Jesus.

There is a place for us to walk where Satan cannot follow. There is a highway, a pathway called the "Highway of Holiness." It's a road strictly reserved for the redeemed to walk on.

> A highway shall be there, and a road,
> And it shall be called the Highway of
>     Holiness.
> The unclean shall not pass over it,
> But it shall be for others.

> Whoever walks the road, although a fool,
> Shall not go astray.
> No lion shall be there,
> Nor shall any ravenous beast go up on it;
> It shall not be found there.
> But the redeemed shall walk there,
> And the ransomed of the LORD shall return,
> And come to Zion with singing,
> With everlasting joy on their heads.
> They shall obtain joy and gladness,
> And sorrow and sighing shall flee away.
>                                   —ISAIAH 35:8–10

Please don't get content with where you are in your relationship with God. Don't let the enemy keep you beneath the weight of these situations in your life. Friend, God wants you to come up the mountain of His presence. There is a place reserved for you where He wants you to sit next to Him. There are things He wants to show you there, and the only way for you to see them is to go up. There are realms of His presence yet to be reached. It's up to you. You determine today where you will walk.

## God Is Looking for You

God has never sought for your worship—He is looking for you. While many today fill the pews, God is still looking for true worshipers in the midst of the crowd. He longs for worshipers who will gather to worship Him, those like the woman with the issue of blood for twelve years who pressed her way through the crowd to touch Jesus. Worship brought her healing (Mark 5:25–34).

God looks for worship to flow from our hearts. God is not moved by the music or the melodies of our songs. God is Spirit. That means He is invisible and can't be seen. While many are trying to impress Him with talent and good music, God is drawn to the worship of our heart. He looks for the unseen worship. The worship God seeks is not found in our style of worship or ability to worship. He is looking for the worship that is being sung deep in our hearts. It has nothing to do with how well you sing or play, but it has everything to do with the condition of your heart while you worship.

> "Now therefore," he said, "put away the foreign gods which are among you, and incline your heart to the LORD God of Israel."
>
> —JOSHUA 24:23

> May He not leave us nor forsake us, that He may incline our hearts to Himself, to walk in all His ways, and to keep His commandments and His statutes and His judgments, which He commanded our fathers.
>
> —1 KINGS 8:57–58

## Worship Must Flow From Our Hearts

For worship to be real, it must be more than just an outward expression such as singing, clapping or lifting our hands. Worship is best described as a picture of God leaning forward as if He is going to kiss you. He bypasses what we are saying with our lips and leans close to incline His ear to our hearts. God listens intently to hear if the worship of our lips lines up with our heart worship. Are both our heart and mouth singing the same song?

# God is looking for the worship that is being sung deep in our hearts.

The invitation to worship is much like being invited to a dance. In worship we have welcomed Him to come, but now God puts out His hand, and you respond. The King desires this dance and every dance with you. He puts out His hand, and you respond. He leans forward for an intimate kiss, and you respond.

At formal, Victorian ballroom dances, the guests had dance cards on which they would write down the names of those for whom each dance was reserved. You have a dance card. Only one name appears on your card—*Jesus*. The Bridegroom has come to dance with you, His bride. Surrounded with light, an unending wedding march envelops you and the Lover of your soul. Together as one, light and music flow from one heart as you and the King dance while the angels watch in wonder.

## Restoring the Altar of Worship

And when Asa heard these words and the prophecy of Oded the prophet, he took courage, and removed the abominable idols from all the land of Judah and Benjamin and from the cities which he had taken in the mountains of Ephraim; and he restored the

altar of the LORD that was before the vestibule
of the LORD.

—2 CHRONICLES 15:8

What a lesson we can learn from this man's journey in restoring the altar of worship. Asa restored the
altar of the Lord. We have built up many altars for the
idols in our hearts. The altar of true worship is a place
of honoring of God. Just as worship needed to be
restored in the days of Asa, God wants to renew true
worship in your heart. When the altar of worship is
restored in our lives, then worship will restore you.

When people worshiped God in the Old and
New Covenant, worship brought restoration and
healing. Worship repairs the damage done by sin.
Worship repairs and renews, because true worship
restores. Restoring the altar of worship will cause
the worshiper to be restored. When you rebuild the
altar of worship, worship will rebuild you. If you
desire for God to repair and restore you, today
repair the altar of your worship. Healing is waiting
for you at the altar! All who entered Jesus' presence
were made whole.

- The leper worshiped and was healed and
  cleansed (Matt. 8:2).

- The ruler's daughter was raised from the
  dead when he worshiped Jesus (Matt.
  9:18, 25).

- The Gentile woman came and worshiped Him, and her demon-possessed
  daughter was delivered and healed
  (Matt. 15:25, 28).

- A demon-possessed man was delivered

when he saw Jesus from afar off, then ran
and worshiped Him (Mark 5:6, 8).

- A blind man worshiped Jesus after he
  was healed (John 9:38).

It's time for you to worship and pray. Dear friend,
God created you to worship Him. But how can we
truly say we have worshiped God when our hearts
are full of so much hurt? It is time for you to move
forward and to go beyond the hurts of the past.
Please, today ask God to remove all the hurt and
pain, all the unseen bitterness and anger that is not
only polluting your heart but also stealing God's
desire and future for you. That bitterness will slowly
and silently kill you.

## God created you to worship Him.

An invitation is being extended to you right now.
God wants to welcome you into His presence. He is
putting out His hand and wants you to respond.
The King wants to dance with you. He puts out His
hand. Will you now respond? He is leaning forward
for an intimate kiss. Will you respond by kissing His
face and asking Him to forgive you? Here in this
intimate place with the King, healing is waiting for
you. A new life can begin right here and now. Just
lean forward with your heart and say, "Yes, Lord, I
am ready for this new relationship with You."

# Afterword

On January 9, 2002, I was ministering at Terry Mahan's. This was during my fast, and I was falling apart because the Lord's presence was so real. I had my eyes closed during worship, just loving His presence. During that time I saw the most beautiful scene of a vision.

> I was standing at the front door of a beautiful big house. A very kind and warm man greeted me at the door and welcomed me to come in. I was overwhelmed by how kind this man was to me. He seemed to be like a king; the house was a palace that words could not describe. I was so overwhelmed by his kindness. Why would he allow me to come in and just be with him? I was thinking this was so kind and warm; what am I doing here? As we walked through the foyer of the house, it was just beautiful, but only to get more beautiful as we came into what looked like a throne room. I just kept asking, "Why I am here? Why has he so welcomed me in? What kind of man is this?"
>
> He then walked toward the throne; he took a couple of steps up and was standing in front of the most beautiful throne I have ever seen. The throne was full of jewels that were set in gold. The color of the gold and

the jewels were like nothing I have ever seen. Now, I was staring at the beauty of the throne and forgot the man who was standing in front of it; the beauty of the throne now became my focus. The man then sat down on the throne and seemed to fade out of my vision, because I was awestruck by the beauty of this throne.

The Lord spoke to me and said, "Don't focus your eyes on the beauty of My Throne. The beauty of the person can so easily be lost in the beauty of the throne. Stay your eyes on Me and not on the throne. As I release new things in your life—My presence, My glory, My power, My blessings—don't focus on those things, but keep your eyes upon Me."

Then the Lord said, "Sam, sow your seeds of worship."

The Lord is receiving seed and sending the harvest of seeds that are being sown in the field of worship. This is where the greatest harvest is coming; the harvest on the seeds sown in the fields of worship will bring back the greatest harvest. There is coming a refreshing in knowing the Holy Spirit—soon!

My friend, I pray that you will fix your eyes on Jesus.

Worship the true and living God with all your heart.

Be refreshed by the Holy Spirit.

Dance with the King.

Kiss His face!

# Notes

## Chapter 1: The Longing Heart

1. Sam Hinn, *Changed in His Presence* (Lake Mary, FL: Charisma House, 1995).

## Chapter 2: What Hinders True Worship?

1. This account of my experience in the service with James Robison is adapted from my earlier book, *Changed in His Presence.*

2. See column one notes in the New King James Version Bible for 1 Corinthians 3:1–4.

## Chapter 6: Show Me Your Glory

1. Biblesoft's New Exhaustive Strong's Numbers and Concordance with Expanded Greek-Hebrew Dictionary. Copyright © 1994, Biblesoft and International Bible Translators, Inc.

## Chapter 10: Created to Worship

1. Over the past five years I have enjoyed reading and compiling information on the light spectrum and the color of sound from many different sources such as the work of Sir Isaac Newton, *Opticks: Treatise of Reflections, Inflections and Colours of Light* (Dover Publishing, 1979) and the Nature of Science Series Physics XI, "The Light Fantastic," *Physics 2000 Explorer Science.*

2. Associated Press, "What Is happening in Science—Sound Waves May Offer Noninvasive Tumor Cure."

3.  Some years ago a friend put a book in my hand titled *Sound of Heaven, Symphony of Earth* by Ray Hughes (MorningStar Publications and Ministries). This book is filled with revelation and insight into worship that ministered so much life to me.

# Other Resources by Sam Hinn

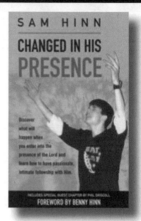

Do you desire to touch the heart of God? Are you seeking intimate fellowship with Him? In *Changed In His Presence*, Sam Hinn uses Scripture and personal experience to show you how to enter into the presence of the Lord through worship.

**Refreshing, live worship CD from The Gathering Place Worship Center**

Experience the presence of the Lord as you worship with these inspired songs that range from contemporary praise to classic hymns and spontaneous worship that touches the heart of God.

## Tape Series

| | |
|---|---|
| Let There be Light | - 4 tapes |
| The Holy Spirit | - 2 tapes |
| Show Me Your Glory | - 2 tapes |
| Dwelling in the Secret Place | - 2 tapes |
| The Glory of Worship | - 2 tapes |
| Living Waters | - 2 tapes |

*many other titles available*

**For a complete catalog of resources and ordering information visit us at:**

## www.samhinn.com

**or write to:**
**Sam Hinn Ministries**
**PO BOX 950596**
**Lake Mary, FL 32795**

# Get Up Close and Personal with God!

# Your Walk With God Can Be Even Deeper...

**W**ith *Charisma* magazine, you'll be informed and inspired by the features and stories about what the Holy Spirit is doing in the lives of believers today.

## Each issue:
- Brings you exclusive world-wide reports to rejoice over.
- Keeps you informed on the latest news from a Christian perspective.
- Includes miracle-filled testimonies to build your faith.
- Gives you access to relevant teaching and exhortation from the most respected Christian leaders of our day.

## Call 1-800-829-3346 for 3 FREE trial issues
Offer #A2CCHB

If you like what you see, then pay the invoice of $22.97 (**saving over 51% off the cover price**) and receive 9 more issues (12 in all). Otherwise, write "cancel" on the invoice, return it, and owe nothing.

## Experience the Power of Spirit-Led Living

*Charisma* Offer #A2CCHB
P.O. Box 420234
Palm Coast, Florida 32142-0234
www.charismamag.com

1884A